ISBN 978-0-483-72355-9
PIBN 10701285

This book is a reproduction of an important historical work. Forgotten Books uses state-of-the-art technology to digitally reconstruct the work, preserving the original format whilst repairing imperfections present in the aged copy. In rare cases, an imperfection in the original, such as a blemish or missing page, may be replicated in our edition. We do, however, repair the vast majority of imperfections successfully; any imperfections that remain are intentionally left to preserve the state of such historical works.

CONTENTS

CONTENTS.

CONTENTS.

THE AGES.

WHEN to the common rest that crowns our
  days,
Called in the noon of life, the good man goes,
Or full of years, and ripe in wisdom, lays
His silver temples in their last repose ; ·
When, o'er the buds of youth, the death-wind
  blows,
And blights the fairest; when our bitterest
  tears
Stream, as the eyes of those that love us
  close,
We think on what they were, with many fears
Lest goodness die with them, and leave the
  coming years.

And therefore, to our hearts, the days gone
  by—
When lived the honored sage whose death
  we wept,
And the soft virtues beamed from many an
  eye,

And beat in many a heart that long has
    slept—
Like spots of earth where angel-feet have
    stepped—
Are holy; and high-dreaming bards have
    told
Of times when worth was crowned, and faith
    was kept,
Ere friendship grew a snare, or love waxed
    cold—
Those pure and happy times—the golden days
    of old.

Peace to the just man's memory,—let it grow
Greener with years, and blossom through the
    flight
Of ages; let the mimic canvas show
His calm benevolent features; let the light
Stream on his deeds of love, that shunned
    the sight
Of all but heaven, and, in the book of fame,
The glorious record of his virtues write,
And hold it up to men, and bid them claim
A palm like his, and catch from him the hal-
    lowed flame.

But oh, despair not of their fate who rise
To dwell upon the earth when we withdraw;

Lo! the same shaft by which the righteous
 dies,
Strikes through the wretch that scoffed at
 mercy's law,
And trode his brethren down, and felt no
 awe
Of Him who will avenge them. Stainless
 worth,
Such as the sternest age of virtue saw,
Ripens, meanwhile, till time shall call it forth
From the low modest shade, to light and bless
 the earth.

Has Nature in her calm, majestic march,
Faltered with age at last? does the bright sun
Grow dim in heaven? or, in their far blue
 arch,
Sparkle the crowd of stars, when day is done,
Less brightly? when the dew-lipped Spring
 comes on,
Breathes she with airs less soft, or scents the
 sky
With flowers less fair than when her reign
 begun?
Does prodigal Autumn, to our age, deny
The plenty that once swelled beneath his sober
 eye?

Look on this beautiful world, and read the
    truth
In her fair page; see, every season brings
New change, to her, of everlasting youth;
Still the green soil, with joyous living things.
Swarms, the wide air is full of joyous wings,
And myriads, still, are happy in the sleep
Of ocean's azure gulfs, and where he flings
The restless surge.   Eternal Love doth keep
In his complacent arms, the earth, the air, the
    deep.

Will then the merciful One, who stamped
    our race
With his own image, and who gave them
    sway
O'er earth, and the glad dwellers on her face,
Now that our flourishing nations far away
Are spread, where'er the moist earth drinks
    the day,
Forget the ancient care that taught and
    nursed
His latest offspring? will he quench the ray
Infused by his own forming smile at first,
And leave a work so fair all blighted and ac-
    cursed?

Oh, no! a thousand cheerful omens give
Hope of yet happier days whose dawn is
    nigh.
He who has tamed the elements, shall not live
The slave of his own passions; he whose eye
Unwinds the eternal dances of the sky,
And in the abyss of brightness dares to span
The sun's broad circle, rising yet more high,
In God's magnificent works his will shall
    scan—
And love and peace shall make their paradise
    with man.

Sit at the feet of History—through the night
Of years the steps of virtue she shall trace,
And show the earlier ages, where her sight
Can pierce the eternal shadows o'er their
    face;—
When from the genial cradle of our race,
Went forth the tribes of men, their pleasant
    lot
To choose, where palm-groves cooled their
    dwelling place,
Or freshening rivers ran; and there forget
The truth of heaven, and kneeled to gods that
    heard them not.

Then waited not the murderer for the night,
But smote his brother down in the bright day,
And he who felt the wrong, and had the
    might,
His own avenger, girt himself to slay;
Beside the path the unburied carcass lay;
The shepherd, by the fountains of the glen,
Fled, while the robber swept his flock away
And slew his babes. The sick, untended
    then,
Languished in the damp shade, and died afar
    from men.

But misery brought in love—in passion's
    strife
Man gave his heart to mercy pleading long,
And sought out gentle deeds to gladden life;
The weak, against the sons of spoil and
    wrong,
Banded, and watched their hamlets, and
    grew strong.
States rose, and, in the shadow of their might,
The timid rested. To the reverent throng,
Grave and time-wrinkled men, with locks all
    white,
Gave laws, and judged their strifes, and taught
    the way of right;

Till bolder spirits seized the rule, and nailed
On men the yoke that man should never
    bear,
And drove them forth to battle: Lo! un-
    veiled
The scene of those stern ages! What is
    there?
A boundless sea of blood, and the wild air
Moans with the crimson surges that entomb
Cities and bannered armies; forms that wear
The kingly circlet, rise amid the gloom,
O'er the dark wave, and straight are swallowed
    in its womb.

Those ages have no memory—but they left
A record in the desert—columns strown
On the waste sands, and statues fall'n and
    cleft,
Heaped like a host in battle overthrown;
Vast ruins, where the mountain's ribs of stone
Were hewn into a city; streets that spread
In the dark earth, where never breath has
    blown
Of heaven's sweet air, nor foot of man dares
    tread
The long and perilous ways—the Cities of
    the Dead:

And tombs of monarchs to the clouds up-
    piled—
They perished—but the eternal tombs re-
    main—
And the black precipice, abrupt and wild,
Pierced by long toil and hollowed to a fane ;—
Hugh piers and frowning forms of gods sus-
    tain
The everlasting arches, dark and wide,
Like the night-heaven when clouds are black
    with rain.
But idly skill was tasked, and strength was
    plied,
All was the work of slaves to swell a despot's
    pride.

And Virtue cannot dwell with slaves, nor
    reign
O'er those who cower to take a tyrant's yoke ;
She left the down-trod nations in disdain,
And flew to Greece, when Liberty awoke,
New-born, amid those beautiful vales, and
    broke
Scepter and chain with her fair youthful
    hands :
As the rock shivers in the thunder-stroke.

And lo! in full-grown strength, an empire
    stands
Of leagued and rival states, the wonder of the
    lands.

Oh, Greece, thy flourishing cities were a
    spoil
Unto each other; thy hard hand oppressed
And crushed the helpless; thou didst make
    thy soil
Drunk with the blood of those that loved
    thee best;
And thou didst drive, from thy unnatural
    breast,
Thy just and brave to die in distant climes;
Earth shuddered at thy deeds, and sighed
    for rest
From thine abominations; after times
That yet shall read thy tale, will tremble at
    thy crimes.

Yet there was that within thee which has
    saved
Thy glory, and redeemed thy blotted name;
The story of thy better deeds, engraved
On fame's unmouldering pillar, puts to shame
Our chiller virtue; the high art to tame

2

The whirlwind of the passions was thine
    own ;
And the pure ray, that from thy bosom came,
Far over many a land and age has shone,
And mingles with the light that beams from
    God's own throne.

And Rome—thy sterner, younger sister, she
Who awed the world with her imperial
    frown—
Rome drew the spirit of her race from thee.—
The rival of thy shame and thy renown.
Yet her degenerate children sold the crown
Of earth's wide kingdoms to a line of slaves ;
Guilt ˙ reigned, and woe with guilt, and
    plagues came down,
Till the north broke its floodgates, and the
    waves
Whelmed the degraded race, and weltered o er
    their graves.

Vainly that ray of brightness from above,
That shone around the Galilean lake,
The light of hope, the leading star of love,
Struggled, the darkness of that day to break ;
Even its own faithless guardians strove to
    slake,

In fogs of earth, the pure immortal flame;
And priestly hands, for Jesus' blessed sake,
Were red with blood, and charity became,
In that stern war of forms, a mockery and a
name.

They triumphed, and less bloody rites were
kept
Within the quiet of the convent cell;
The well-fed inmates pattered prayer, and
slept,
And sinned, and liked their easy penance
well.
Where pleasant was the spot for men to
dwell,
Amid its fair broad lands the abbey lay,
Sheltering dark orgies that were shame to
tell,
And cowled and barefoot beggars swarmed
the way.
All in their convent weeds, of black, and
white, and gray.

Oh, sweetly the returning muses' strain
Swelled over that famed stream, whose gen-
tle tide
In their bright lap the Etrurian vales detain,

Sweet, as when winter storms have ceased to
    chide,
And all the new-leaved woods, resounding
    wide,
Send out wild hymns upon the scented air.
Lo ! to the smiling Arno's classic side
The emulous nations of the west repair,
And kindle their quenched urns, and drink
    fresh spirit there.

Still, Heaven deferred the hour ordained to
    rend
From saintly rottenness the sacred stole ;
And cowl and worshipped shrine could still
    defend
The wretch with felon stains upon his soul ;
And crimes were set to sale, and hard his
    dole
Who could not bribe a passage to the skies ;
And vice, beneath the mitre's kind control,
Sinned gayly on, and grew to giant size,
Shielded by priestly power, and watched by
    priestly eyes.

At last the earthquake came—the shock,
    that hurled
To dust, in many fragments dashed and
    strown,

The throne. whose roots were in another
    world,
And whose far-stretching shadow awed our
    own.
From many a proud monastic pile, o'erthrown,
Fear-struck, the hooded inmates rushed and
    fled ;
The web, that for a thousand years had
    grown
O'er prostrate Europe, in that day of dread
Crumbled and fell, as fire dissolves the flaxen
    thread.

The spirit of that day is still awake,
And spreads himself, and shall not sleep
    again ;
But through the idle mesh of power shall
    break,
Like billows o'er the Asian monarch's chain ;
Till men are filled with him, and feel how
    vain,
Instead of the pure heart and innocent hands,
Are all the proud and pompous modes to
    gain
The smile of heaven ;--till a new age expands
Its white and holy wings above the peaceful
    lands.

For look again on the past years ;—behold,
Flown, like the nightmare's hideous shapes,
    away,
Full many a horrible worship, that, of old,
Held, o'er the shuddering realms, unques-
    tioned sway :
See crimes that feared not once the eye of
    day,
Rooted from men, without a name or place :
See nations blotted out from earth, to pay
The forfeit of deep guilt ;—with glad embrace
The fair disburdened lands welcome a noble
    race.

Thus error's monstrous shapes from earth are
    driven,
They fade, they fly,—but truth survives their
    flight ;
Earth has no shades to quench that beam of,
    heaven ;
Each ray, that shone, in early time, to light
The faltering footsteps in the path of right,
Each gleam of clearer brightness, shed to aid
In man's maturer day his bolder sight,
All blended, like the rainbow's radiant braid,
Pour yet, and still shall pour, the blaze that
    cannot fade.

Late, from this western shore, that morning
    chased
The deep and ancient night, that threw its
    shroud
O'er the green land of groves, the beautiful
    waste,
Nurse of full streams, and lifter up of proud
Sky-mingling mountains that o'erlook the
    cloud.
Erewhile, where yon gay spires their bright-
    ness rear,
Trees waved, and the brown hunter's shouts
    were loud
Amid the forest : and the bounding deer
Fled at the glancing plume, and the gaunt wolf
    yelled near.

And where his willing waves yon bright blue
    bay
Sends up to kiss his decorated brim,
And cradles, in his soft embrace, the gay
Young group of grassy islands born of him,
And crowding nigh, or in the distance dim,
Lifts the white throng of sails, that bear or
    bring
The commerce of the world ;—with tawny
    limb,

And belt and beads in sunlight glistening,
The savage urged his skiff like wild bird on the
    wing.

Then, all this youthful paradise around,
And all the broad and boundless mainland,
    lay
Cooled by the interminable wood, that
    frowned
O'er mount and vale, where never summer
    ray
Glanced, till the strong tornado broke his
    way
Through the gray giants of the sylvan wild;
Yet many a sheltered glade, with blossoms
    gay,
Beneath the showery sky and sunshine mild,
Within the shaggy arms of that dark forest
    smiled.

There stood the Indian hamlet, there the lake
Spread its blue sheet that flashed with many
    an oar,
Where the brown otter plunged him from the
    brake,
And the deer drank: as the light gale flew
    o'er,

The twinkling maize-field rustled on the
shore;
And while that spot, so wild, and lone, and
fair,
A look of glad and innocent beauty wore,
And peace was on the earth and in the air,
The warrior lit the pile, and bound his captive
there:

Not unavenged—the foeman, from the wood,
Beheld the deed, and when the midnight
shade
Was stillest, gorged his battle-axe with blood;
All died—the wailing babe—the shrieking
maid—
And in the flood of fire that scathed the
glade,
The roofs went down; but deep the silence
grew,
When on the dewy woods the day-beam
played;
No more the cabin smokes rose wreathed
and blue,
And ever, by their lake, lay moored the light
canoe.

Look now abroad—another race has filled
These populous borders—wide the wood re-
    cedes,
And towns shoot up, and fertile realms are
    tilled;
The land is full of harvests and green meads;
Streams numberless, that many a fountain
    feeds,
Shine, disembowered, and give to sun and
    breeze
Their virgin waters; the full region leads
New colonies forth, that toward the western
    seas
Spread, like a rapid flame among the autumnal
    trees.

Here the free spirit of mankind, at length,
Throws its last fetters off; and who shall
    place
A limit to the giant's unchained strength,
Or curb his swiftness in the forward race?
Far, like the comet's way through infinite
    space,
Stretches the long untravelled path of light
Into the depths of ages: we may trace,
Distant, the brightening glory of its light,
Till the receding rays are lost to human sight.

Europe is given a prey to sterner fates,
And writhes in shackles; strong the arms
　　that chain
To earth her struggling multitude of states:
She too is strong, and might not chafe in
　　vain
Against them, but shake off the vampyre
　　train
That batten on her blood, and break their
　　net.
Yes, she shall look on brighter days, and gain
The meed of worthier deeds; the moment set
To rescue and raise up, draws near—but is not
　　yet.

But thou, my country, thou shalt never fall,
But with thy children—thy maternal care,
Thy lavish love, thy blessings showered on
　　all—
These are thy fetters—seas and stormy air
Are the wide barrier of thy borders, where,
Among thy gallant sons that guard thee well,
Thou laugh'st at enemies: who shall then
　　declare
The date of thy deep-founded strength, or
　　tell
How happy, in thy lap, the sons of men shall
　　dwell?

TO THE PAST.

Thou unrelenting Past!
Strong are the barriers round thy dark domain,
　And fetters, sure and fast,
Hold all that enter thy unbreathing reign.

　Far in thy realm withdrawn
Old empires sit in sullenness and gloom,
　And glorious ages gone
Lie deep within the shadow of thy womb.

　Childhood, with all its mirth,
Youth, Manhood, Age, that draws us to the
　　ground,
　And last, Man's Life on earth,
Glide to thy dim dominions, and are bound.

　Thou hast my better years,
Thou hast my earlier friends—the good—the
　　kind,
　Yielded to thee with tears—
The venerable form—the exalted mind.

　My spirit yearns to bring
The lost ones back—yearns with desire intense,
　And struggles hard to wring
Thy bolts apart, and pluck thy captives thence.

In vain—thy gates deny
All passage save to those who hence depart ;
  Nor to the streaming eye
Thou giv'st them back—nor to the broken heart.

  In thy abysses hide
Beauty and excellence unknown—to thee
  Earth's wonder and her pride
Are gathered, as the waters to the sea ;

  Labors of good to man,
Unpublished charity, unbroken faith,—
  Love, that midst grief began,
And grew with years, and faltered not in death.

  Full many a mighty name
Lurks in thy depths, unuttered, unrevered ;
  With thee are silent fame,
Forgotten arts, and wisdom disappeared.

  Thine for a space are they—
Yet shalt thou yield thy treasures up at last !
  Thy gates shall yet give way,
Thy bolts shall fall, inexorable Past !

  All that of good and fair
Has gone into thy womb from earliest time,
  Shall then come forth, to wear
The glory and the beauty of its prime.

They have not perished—no!
Kind words, remembered voices once so sweet,
  Smiles, radiant long ago,
And features, the great soul's apparent seat;

  All shall come back, each tie
Of pure affection shall be knit again;
  Alone shall Evil die,
And Sorrow dwell a prisoner in thy reign.

  And then, shall I behold
Him, by whose kind paternal side I sprung,
  And her, who, still and cold,
Fills the next grave—the beautiful and young.

THANATOPSIS.

To him who in the love of nature holds
Communion with her visible forms, she speaks
A various language; for his gayer hours
She has a voice of gladness, and a smile
And eloquence of beauty, and she glides
Into his darker musings, with a mild
And healing sympathy, that steals away
Their sharpness, ere he is aware.   When
    thoughts
Of the last bitter hour come like a blight

Over thy spirit, and sad images
Of the stern agony, and shroud, and pall,
And breathless darkness, and the narrow house,
Make thee to shudder, and grow sick at heart ;—
Go forth, under the open sky, and list
To Nature's teachings, while from all around—
Earth and her waters, and the depths of air,—
Comes a still voice—Yet a few days, and thee
The all-beholding sun shall see no more
In all his course ; nor yet in the cold ground,
Where thy pale form was laid, with many tears,
Nor in the embrace of ocean, shall exist
Thy image.   Earth, that nourished thee, shall
    claim
Thy growth, to be resolved to earth again,
And, lost each human trace, surrendering up
Thine individual being, shalt thou go
To mix forever with the elements,
To be a brother to the insensible rock
And to the sluggish clod, which the rude swain
Turns with his share, and treads upon.   The
    oak
Shall send his roots abroad, and pierce thy
    mould.
Yet not to thine eternal resting-place
Shalt thou retire alone—nor couldst thou wish
Couch more magnificent.   Thou shalt lie down

With patriarchs of the infant world—with kings,
The powerful of the earth—the wise, the good,
Fair forms, and hoary seers of ages past,
All in one mighty sepulchre.—The hills
Rock-ribbed and ancient as the sun,—the vales
Stretching in pensive quietness between;
The venerable woods—rivers that move
In majesty, and the complaining brooks
That make the meadows green; and, poured
    round all,
Old ocean's gray and melancholy waste,—
Are but the solemn decorations all
Of the great tomb of man.   The golden sun,
The planets, all the infinite host of heaven,
Are shining on the sad abodes of death,
Through the still lapse of ages.   All that tread
The globe are but a handful to the tribes
That slumber in its bosom.—Take the wings
Of morning—and the Barcan desert pierce,
Or lose thyself in the continuous woods
Where rolls the Oregan, and hears no sound,
Save his own dashings—yet—the dead are
    there;
And millions in those solitudes, since first
The flight of years began, have laid them down
In their last sleep—the dead reign there alone.
So shalt thou rest—and what if thou withdraw

Unheeded by the living—and no friend
Take note of thy departure? All that breathe
Will snare thy destiny. The gay will laugh
When thou art gone, the solemn brood of care
Plod on, and each one as before will chase
His favorite phantom ; yet all these shall leave
Their mirth and their employments, and shall come,
And make their bed with thee. As the long train
Of ages glide away, the sons of men,
The youth in life's green spring, and he who goes
In the full strength of years, matron, and maid,
And the sweet babe, and the gray-headed man,—
Shall one by one be gathered to thy side,
By those, who in their turn shall follow them.

So live, that when thy summons comes to join
The innumerable caravan, that moves
To that mysterious realm, where each shall take
His chamber in the silent halls of death,
Thou go not, like the quarry-slave at night,
Scourged to his dungeon, but, sustained and soothed
By an unfaltering trust, approach thy grave,
Like one who wraps the drapery of his couch
About him, and lies down to pleasant dreams.

THE LAPSE OF TIME.

LAMENT who will, in fruitless tears,
　　The speed with which our moments fly:
I sigh not over vanished years,
　　But watch the years that hasten by.

Look, how they come,—a mingled crowd
　　Of bright and dark, but rapid days;
Beneath them, like a summer cloud,
　　The wide world changes as I gaze.

What! grieve that time has brought so soon
　　The sober age of manhood on?
As idly might I weep, at noon,
　　To see the blush of morning gone.

Could I give up the hopes that glow
　　In prospect, like Elysian isles;
And let the charming future go,
　　With all her promises and smiles?

The future!—cruel were the power
　　Whose doom would tear thee from my heart,
Thou sweetener of the present hour!
　　We cannot—no—we will not part.

Oh, leave me, still, the rapid flight
  That makes the changing seasons gay,
The grateful speed that brings the night,
  The swift and glad return of day;

The months that touch, with added grace,
  This little prattler at my knee,
In whose arch eye and speaking face
  New meaning every hour I see;

The years, that o'er each sister land
  Shall lift the country of my birth
And nurse her strength, till she shall stand
  The pride and pattern of the earth;

Till younger commonwealths, for aid,
  Shall cling about her ample robe,
And from her frown shall shrink afraid
  The crowned oppressors of the globe.

True—time will seam and blanch my brow—
  Well—I shall sit with aged men,
And my good glass will tell me how
  A grizzly beard becomes me then.

And should no foul dishonor lie
  Upon my head, when I am gray,
Love yet shall watch my fading eye,
  And smooth the path of my decay.

Then, haste thee, Time—'tis kindness all
  That speeds thy winged feet so fast;
Thy pleasures stay not till they pall,
  And all thy pains are quickly past.

Thou fliest and bear'st away our woes,
  And as thy shadowy train depart,
The memory of sorrow grows
  A lighter burden on the heart.

TO THE EVENING WIND.

Spirit that breathest through my lattice, thou
  That cool'st the twilight of the sultry day,
Gratefully flows thy freshness round my brow;
  Thou hast been out upon the deep at play,
Riding all day the wild blue waves till now,
    Roughening their crests, and scattering high
      their spray,
And swelling the white sail.   I welcome thee
To the scorched land, thou wanderer of the
    sea!

Nor I alone—a thousand bosoms round
   Inhale thee in the fulness of delight;
And languid forms rise up, and pulses bound
   Livelier, at coming of the wind of night;
And, languishing to hear thy grateful sound,
   Lies the vast inland stretched beyond the sight.
Go forth into the gathering shade; go forth,
God's blessing breathed upon the fainting earth!

Go, rock the little wood-bird in his nest,
   Curl the still waters, bright with stars, and
     rouse
The wide old wood from his majestic rest,
   Summoning from the innumerable boughs
The strange, deep harmonies that haunt his
     breast:
   Pleasant shall be thy way where meekly
     bows
The shutting flower, and darkling waters pass,
And 'twixt the o'ershadowing branches and
     the grass.

The faint old man shall lean his silver head
   To feel thee; thou shalt kiss the child asleep,
And dry the moistened curls that overspread
   His temples, while his breathing grows more
     deep;

And they who stand about the sick man's bed,
  Shall joy to listen to thy distant sweep,
And softly part his curtains to allow
Thy visit, grateful to his burning brow.

Go—but the circle of eternal change,
  Which is the life of nature, shall restore,
With sounds and scents from all thy mighty
    range,
    Thee to thy birthplace of the deep once
    more ;
Sweet odors in the sea-air, sweet and strange,
  Shall tell the home-sick mariner of the shore;
And, listening to thy murmur, he shall deem
He hears the rustling leaf and running stream.

FOREST HYMN.

THE groves were God's first temples. Ere
  man learned
To hew the shaft, and lay the architrave,
And spread the roof above them,—ere he
  framed
The lofty vault, to gather and roll back
The sound of anthems ; in the darkling wood,
Amidst the cool and silence, he knelt down
And offered to the Mightiest, solemn thanks

And supplication.   For his simple heart
Might not resist the sacred influences,
Which, from the stilly twilight of the place,
And from the gray old trunks that high in
    heaven
Mingled their mossy boughs, and from the
    sound
Of the invisible breath that swayed at once
All their green tops, stole over him, and bowed
His spirit with the thought of boundless power
And inaccessible majesty.   Ah, why
Should we, in the world's riper years, neglect
God's ancient sanctuaries, and adore
Only among the crowd, and under roofs
That our frail hands have raised?   Let me, at
    least,
Here, in the shadow of this aged wood,
Offer one hymn—thrice happy, if it find
Acceptance in His ear.

                              Father, thy hand
Hath reared these venerable columns, thou
Didst weave this verdant roof.   Thou didst
    look down
Upon the naked earth, and, forthwith, rose
All these fair ranks of trees.   They, in thy sun,

Budded, and shook their green leaves in thy
    breeze,
And shot toward heaven. The century-living
    crow
Whose birth was in their tops, grew old and
    died
Among their branches, till, at last, they stood,
As now they stand, massy, and tall, and dark,
Fit shrine for humble worshipper to hold
Communion with his Maker. These dim vaults
These winding isles, of human pomp or pride
Report not. No fantastic carvings show,
The boast of our vain race to change the form
Of thy fair works. But thou art here—thou
    fill'st
The solitude. Thou art in the soft winds
That run along the summit of these trees
In music;—thou art in the cooler breath,
That from the inmost darkness of the place,
Comes, scarcely felt;—the barky trunks, the
    ground,
The fresh moist ground, are all instinct with
    thee.
Here is continual worship;—nature, here,
In the tranquillity that thou dost love,
Enjoys thy presence. Noiselessly, around,
From perch to perch, the solitary bird

Passes; and yon clear spring, that, 'midst its
    herbs,
Wells softly forth and visits the strong roots
Of half the mighty forest, tells no tale
Of all the good it does.   Thou hast not left
Thyself without a witness, in these shades,
Of thy perfections.   Grandeur, strength and
    grace
Are here to speak of thee.   This mighty oak—
By whose immovable stem I stand and seem
Almost annihilated—not a prince,
In all that proud old world beyond the deep,
E'er wore his crown as loftily as he
Wears the green coronal of leaves with which
Thy hand has graced him.   Nestled at his
    root
Is beauty, such as blooms not in the glare
Of the broad sun.   That delicate forest flower,
With scented breath, and look so like a smile,
Seems, as it issues from the shapeless mould,
An emanation of the indwelling Life,
A visible token of the upholding Love,
That are the soul of this wide universe.

   My heart is awed within me, when I think
Of the great miracle that still goes on,
In silence, round me—the perpetual work

Of thy creation, finished, yet renewed
Forever.   Written on thy works I read
The lesson of thy own eternity.
Lo! all grow old and die—but see, again,
How on the faltering footsteps of decay
Youth presses—ever gay and beautiful youth
In all its beautiful forms.   These lofty trees
Wave not less proudly that their ancestors
Moulder beneath them.   Oh, there is not lost
One of earth's charms: upon her bosom yet,
After the flight of untold centuries,
The freshness of her far beginning lies
And yet shall lie.   Life mocks the idle hate
Of his arch enemy Death—yea, seats himself
Upon the tyrant's throne—the sepulchre,
And of the triumphs of his ghastly foe
Makes his own nourishment.   For he came
    forth
From thine own bosom, and shall have no end.

There have been holy men who hid them-
    selves
Deep in the woody wilderness, and gave
Their lives to thought and prayer, till they out-
    lived
The generation born with them, nor seemed
Less aged than the hoary trees and rocks

Around them ;—and there have been holy men
Who deemed it were not well to pass life thus.
But let me often to these solitudes
Retire, and in thy presence reassure
My feeble virtue.   Here its enemies,
The passions, at thy plainer footsteps shrink
And tremble and are still.   Oh, God ! when
    thou
Dost scare the world with tempests, set on fire
The heavens with falling thunderbolts, or fill,
With all the waters of the firmament,
The swift dark whirlwind that uproots the
    woods
And drowns the villages ; when, at thy call,
Uprises the great deep and throws himself
Upon the continent, and overwhelms
Its cities—who forgets not, at the sight
Of these tremendous tokens of thy power,
His pride, and lays his strifes and follies by ?
Oh, from these sterner aspects of thy face
Spare me and mine, nor let us need the wrath
Of the mad unchained elements to teach
Who rules them.   Be it ours to meditate
In these calm shades thy milder majesty,
And to the beautiful order of thy works,
Learn to conform the order of our lives.

THE OLD MAN'S FUNERAL.

I SAW an aged man upon his bier,
　His hair was thin and white, and on his brow
A record of the cares of many a year;—
　Cares that were ended and forgotten now.
And there was sadness round, and faces bowed,
And women's tears fell fast, and children
　wailed aloud.

Then rose another hoary man and said,
　In faltering accents, to that weeping train,
" Why mourn ye that our aged friend is dead ?
　Ye are not sad to see the gathered grain,
Nor when their mellow fruit the orchards cast,
Nor when the yellow woods shake down the
　ripened mast.

" Ye sigh not when the sun, his course fulfilled,
　His glorious course, rejoicing earth and sky;
In the soft evening, when the winds are stilled,
　Sinks where his islands of refreshment lie,
And leaves the smile of his departure, spread
O'er the warm-colored heaven and ruddy
　mountain head.

" Why weep ye then for him, who, having won
　The bound of man's appointed years, at last,

Life's blessings all enjoyed, life's labors done,
　Serenely to his final rest has passed
While the soft memory of his virtues, yet,
Lingers like twilight hues, when the bright sun
　　is set.

" His youth was innocent; his riper age,
　Marked with some act of goodness, every
　　day ;
And watched by eyes that loved him, calm,
　　and sage,
　Faded his late declining years away.
Cheerful he gave his being up, and went
To share the holy rest that waits a life well
　　spent.

" That life was happy ; every day he gave
　Thanks for the fair existence that was his ;
For a sick fancy made him not her slave,
　To mock him with her phantom miseries.
No chronic tortures racked his aged limb,
For luxury and sloth had nourished none for
　　him.

" And I am glad that he has lived thus long,
　And glad, that he has gone to his reward ;

Nor deem, that kindly nature did him wrong,
  Softly to disengage the vital cord.
When his weak hand grew palsied, and his eye
Dark with the mists of age, it was his time to
    die."

THE *PRAIRIES.*

THESE are the Gardens of the Desert, these
The unshorn fields, boundless and beautiful,
For which the speech of England has no
    name—
The Prairies.   I behold them for the first,
And my heart swells, while the dilated sight
Takes in the encircling vastness.   Lo! they
    stretch
In airy undulations, far away,
As if the ocean, in his gentlest swell,
Stood still, with all his rounded billows fixed,
And motionless forever.—Motionless?—
No—they are all unchained again. The clouds
Sweep over with their shadows, and, beneath,
The surface rolls and fluctuates to the eye;
Dark hollows seem to glide along and chase
The sunny ridges.   Breezes of the South!
Who toss the golden and the flame-like flowers,
And pass the prairie-hawk that, poised on high,

Flaps his broad wings, yet moves not—ye have
　　played
Among the palms of Mexico and vines
Of Texas, and have crisped the limpid brooks
That from the fountains of Sonora glide
Into the calm Pacific—have ye fanned
A nobler or a lovelier scene than this?
Man hath no part in all this glorious work:
The hand that built the firmament hath heaved
And smoothed these verdant swells, and sown
　　their slopes
With herbage, planted them with island groves,
And hedged them round with forests.　Fitting
　　floor
For this magnificent temple of the sky—
With flowers whose glory and whose multitude
Rival the constellations!　The great heavens
Seem to stoop down upon the scene in love,—
A nearer vault, and of a tenderer blue,
Than that which bends above the eastern hills.

As o'er the verdant waste I guide my steed,
Among the high rank grass that sweeps his
　　sides,
The hollow beating of his footsteps seems
A sacrilegious sound.　I think of those
Upon whose rest he tramples.　Are they here—

The dead of other days ?—and did the dust
Of these fair solitudes once stir with life
And burn with passion?   Let the mighty
        mounds
That overlook the rivers, or that rise
In the dim forest crowded with old oaks,
Answer.   A race, that long has passed away,
Built them ;— a disciplined and populous race
Heaped, with long toil, the earth, while yet the
        Greek
Was hewing the Pentelicus to forms
Of symmetry, and rearing on its rock
The glittering Parthenon.   These ample fields
Nourished their harvests, here their herds were
        fed,
When haply by their stalls the bison lowed,
And bowed his maned shoulder to the yoke.
All day this desert murmured with their toils,
Till twilight blushed and lovers walked, and
        wooed
In a forgotten language, and old tunes,
From instruments of unremembered form,
Gave the soft winds a voice.   The red man
        came—
The roaming hunter tribes, warlike and fierce,
And the mound-builders vanished from the
        earth.

The solitude of centuries untold
Has settled where they dwelt. The prairie wolf
Hunts in their meadows, and his fresh-dug den
Yawns by my path. The gopher mines the
    ground
Where stood their swarming cities. All is
    gone—
All—save the piles of earth that hold their
    bones—
The platforms where they worshipped unknown
    gods—
The barriers which they builded from the soil
To keep the foe at bay—till o'er the walls
The wild beleaguers broke, and, one by one,
The strongholds of the plain were forced and
    heaped
With corpses. The brown vultures of the wood
Flocked to those vast uncovered sepulchres,
And sat, unscared and silent, at their feast.
Haply some solitary fugitive,
Lurking in marsh and forest, till the sense
Of desolation and of fear became
Bitterer than death, yielded himself to die.
Man's better nature triumphed. Kindly words
Welcomed and soothed him; the rude con-
    querors
Seated the captive with their chiefs; he chose

A bride among their maidens, and at length
Seemed to forget,—yet ne'er forgot,—the wife
Of his first love, and her sweet little ones
Butchered amid their shrieks, with all his race.
    Thus change the forms of being. Thus arise
Races of living things, glorious in strength,
And perish, as the quickening breath of God
Fills them, or is withdrawn. The red man
    too—
Has left the blooming wilds he ranged so long,
And, near to the Rocky Mountains, sought
A wider hunting-ground. The beaver builds
No longer by these streams, but far away,
On waters whose blue surface ne'er gave back
The white man's face—among Missouri's
    springs,
And pools whose issues swell the Oregan,
He rears his little Venice. In these plains
The bison feeds no more. Twice twenty leagues
Beyond remotest smoke of hunter's camp,
Roams the majestic brute, in herds that shake
The earth with thundering steps—yet here I
    meet
His ancient footprints stamped beside the pool.
    Still this great solitude is quick with life.
Myriads of insects, gaudy as the flowers
They flutter over, gentle quadrupeds,

And birds, that scarce have learned the fear of
    man,
Are here, and sliding reptiles of the ground,
Startlingly beautiful.   The graceful deer
Bounds to the wood at my approach. The bee,
A more adventurous colonist than man,
With whom he came across the eastern deep,
Fills the savannas with his murmurings,
And hides his sweets, as in the golden age,
Within the hollow oak.   I listen long
To his domestic hum, and think I hear
The sound of that advancing multitude
Which soon shall fill these deserts.   From the
    ground
Comes up the laugh of children, the soft voice
Of maidens, and the sweet and solemn hymn
Of Sabbath worshippers.   The low of herds
Blends with the rustling of the heavy grain
Over the dark-brown furrows.   All at once
A fresher wind sweeps by, and breaks my
    dream,
And I am in the wilderness alone.

THE KNIGHT'S EPITAPH.

THIS is the church which Pisa, great and free,
Reared to St. Catharine. How the time-stained
    walls,

That earthquakes shook not from their poise,
    appear
To shiver in the deep and voluble tones
Rolled from the organ! Underneath my feet
There lies the lid of a sepulchral vault.
The image of an armed knight is graven
Upon it, clad in perfect panoply—
Cuishes, and greaves, and cuirass, with barred
    helm,
Gauntleted hand, and sword, and blazoned
    shield.
Around, in Gothic characters, worn dim
By feet of worshippers, are traced his name,
And birth, and death, and words of eulogy.
Why should I pore upon them? This old tomb,
This effigy, the strange disused form
Of this inscription, eloquently show
His history. Let me clothe in fitting words
The thoughts they breathe, and frame his
    epitaph.

" He whose forgotten dust for centuries
Has lain beneath this stone, was one in whom
Adventure, and endurance, and emprise
Exalted the mind's faculties and strung
The body's sinews. Brave he was in fight,
Courteous in banquet, scornful of repose,

And bountiful, and cruel, and devout,
And quick to draw the sword in private feud.
He pushed his quarrels to the death, yet prayed
The saints as fervently on bended knees
As ever shaven cenobite. He loved
As fiercely as he fought. He would have borne
The maid that pleased him from her bower by
    night,
To his hill-castle, as the eagle bears
His victim from the fold, and rolled the rocks
On his pursuers. He aspired to see
His native Pisa queen and arbitress
Of cities; earnestly for her he raised
His voice in council, and affronted death
In battle-field, and climbed the galley's deck,
And brought the captured flag of Genoa back,
Or piled upon the Arno's crowded quay
The glittering spoils of the tamed Saracen.
He was not born to brook the stranger's yoke,
But would have joined the exiles, that withdrew
For ever, when the Florentine broke in
The gates of Pisa, and bore off the bolts
For trophies—but he died before that day.

    " He lived, the impersonation of an age
That never shall return. His soul of fire
Was kindled by the breath of the rude time

He lived in.   Now a gentler race succeeds,
Shuddering at blood; the effeminate cavalier,
Turning from the reproaches of the past,
And from the hopeless future, gives to ease,
And love and music, his inglorious life."

SEVENTY–SIX.

WHAT heroes from the woodland sprung,
   When, through the fresh awakened land,
The thrilling cry of freedom rung,
And to the work of warfare strung
   The yoeman's iron hand!

Hills flung the cry to hills around,
   And ocean-mart replied to mart,
And streams, whose springs were yet unfound,
Pealed far away the startling sound
   Into the forest's heart.

Then marched the brave from rocky steep,
   From mountain river swift and cold;
The borders of the stormy deep,
The vales where gathered waters sleep,
   Sent up the strong and bold,—

As if the very earth again
  Grew quick with God's creating breath,
And, from the sods of grove and glen,
Rose ranks of lion-hearted men
  To battle to the death.

The wife, whose babe first smiled that day,
  The fair fond bride of yestereve,
And aged sire and matron gray,
Saw the loved warriors haste away,
  And deemed it sin to grieve.

Already had the strife begun ;
  Already blood on Concord's plain
Along the springing grass had run,
And blood had flowed at Lexington,
  Like brooks of April rain.

That death-stain on the vernal sward
  Hallowed to freedom all the shore ;
In fragments fell the yoke abhorred—
The footstep of a foreign lord
  Profaned the soil no more.

THE HUNTER OF THE PRAIRIES.

Ay this is freedom!—these pure skies
  Were never stained with village smoke:
The fragrant wind, that through them flies,
  Is breathed from wastes by plough unbroke.
Here, with my rifle and my steed,
  And her who left the world for me,
I plant me, where the red deer feed
  In the green desert—and am free.

For here the fair savannas know
  No barriers in the bloomy grass;
Wherever breeze of heaven may blow,
  Or beam of heaven may glance, I pass.
In pastures, measureless as air,
  The bison is my noble game;
The bounding elk, whose antlers tear
  The branches, falls before my aim.

Mine are the river-fowl that scream
  From the long stripe of waving sedge;
The bear, that marks my weapon's gleam,
  Hides vainly in the forest's edge;
In vain the she-wolf stands at bay;
  The brinded catamount, that lies
High in the boughs to watch his prey,
  Even in the act of springing, dies.

With what free growth the elm and plane
　Fling their huge arms across my way,
Gray, old, and cumbered with a train
　Of vines, as huge, and old, and gray!
Free stray the lucid streams, and find
　No taint in these fresh lawns and shades :
Free spring the flowers that scent the wind
　Where never scythe has swept the glades.

Alone the Fire, when frostwinds sere
　The heavy herbage of the ground,
Gathers his annual harvest here,
　With roaring like the battle's sound,
And hurrying flames that sweep the plain,
　And smoke-streams gushing up the sky:
I meet the flames with flames again,
　And at my door they cower and die.

Here, from dim woods, the aged past
　Speaks solemnly; and I behold
The boundless future in the vast
　And lonely river, seaward rolled.
Who feeds its founts with rain and dew?
　Who moves, I ask, its gliding mass,
And trains the bordering vines, whose blue
　Bright clusters tempt me as I pass?

Broad are these streams—my steed obeys,
  Plunges, and bears me through the tide.
Wide are these woods—I thread the maze
  Of giant stems, nor ask a guide.
I hunt, till day's last glimmer dies
  O'er woody vale and grassy height;
And kind the voice and glad the eyes,
  That welcome my return at night.

A SONG OF PITCAIRN'S ISLAND.

COME, take our boy, and we will go
  Before our cabin door;
The winds shall bring us, as they blow,
  The murmurs of the shore;
And we will kiss his young blue eyes,
And I will sing him, as he lies,
  Songs that were made of yore:
I'll sing, in his delighted ear,
The island lays thou lov'st to hear.

And thou, while stammering I repeat,
  Thy country's tongue shalt teach;
'Tis not so soft, but far more sweet,
  Than my own native speech:
For thou no other tongue didst know,

When, scarcely twenty moons ago,
   Upon Tahete's beach,
Thou cam'st to woo me to be thine,
With many a speaking look and sign.

I knew thy meaning—thou didst praise
   My eyes, my locks of jet;
Ah! well for me they won thy gaze,—
   But thine were fairer yet!
I'm glad to see my infant wear
Thy soft blue eyes and sunny hair,
   And when my sight is met
By his white brow and blooming cheek,
I feel a joy I cannot speak.

Come talk of Europe's maids with me,
   Whose necks and cheeks, they tell,
Outshine the beauty of the sea,
   White foam and crimson shell.
I'll shape like theirs my simple dress,
And bind like them each jetty tress,
   A sight to please thee well:
And for my dusky brow will braid
A bonnet like an English maid.

Come, for the soft low sunlight calls,
   We lose the pleasant hours;

'Tis lovelier than these cottage walls,—
　That seat among the flowers.
And I will learn of thee a prayer,
To Him, who gave a home so fair,
　A lot so blessed as ours—
The God who made, for thee and me,
This sweet lone isle amid the sea.

RIZPAH.

And he delivered them into the hands of the Gibeonites, and they hanged them in the hill before the Lord ; and they fell all seven together, and were put to death in the days of the harvest, in the first days, in the beginning of barley-harvest.

And Rizpah, the daughter of Aiah, took sackcloth, and spread it for her upon the rock, from the beginning of harvest until the water dropped upon them out of heaven, and suffered neither the birds of the air to rest upon them by day, nor the beasts of the field by night.—2 SAM. xxi. 10.

HEAR what the desolate Rizpah said,
As on Gibeah's rocks she watched the dead.
The sons of Michal before her lay,
And her own fair children dearer than they:
By a death of shame they all had died,
And were stretched on the bare rock, side by
　　side.
And Rizpah, once the loveliest of all

That bloomed and smiled in the court of Saul,
All wasted with watching and famine now,
And scorched by the sun her haggard brow,
Sat, mournfully guarding their corpses there,
And murmured a strange and solemn air;
The low, heart-broken, and wailing strain
Of a mother that mourns her children slain.

" I have made the crags my home, and spread
On their desert backs my sackcloth bed;
I have eaten the bitter herb of the rocks,
And drunk the midnight dew in my locks;
I have wept till I could not weep, and the pain
Of my burning eyeballs went to my brain.
Seven blackened corpses before me lie,
In the blaze of the sun and the winds of the
    sky.
I have watched them through the burning day
And driven the vulture and raven away;
And the cormorant wheeled in circles round,
Yet feared to alight on the guarded ground.
And, when the shadows of twilight came,
I have seen the hyena's eyes of flame,
And heard at my side his stealthy tread,
But aye at my shout the savage fled:
And I threw the lighted brand, to fright
The jackal and wolf that yelled in the night.

"Ye were foully murdered, my hapless sons,
By the hands of wicked and cruel ones;
Ye fell, in your fresh and blooming prime,
All innocent, for your father's crime.
He sinned—but he paid the price of his guilt
When his blood by a nameless hand was spilt;
When he strove with the heathen host in vain,
And fell with the flower of his people slain,
And the sceptre his children's hands should
    sway
From his injured lineage passed away.

"But I hoped that the cottage roof would be
A safe retreat for my sons and me;
And that while they ripened to manhood fast,
They should wean my thoughts from the woes
    of the past.
And my bosom swelled with a mother's pride,
As they stood in their beauty and strength by
    my side,
Tall like their sire, with the princely grace
Of his stately form, and the bloom of his face.

"Oh, what an hour for a mother's heart,
When the pitiless ruffians tore us apart!
When I clasped their knees and wept and
    prayed,

And struggled and shrieked to Heaven for aid,
And clung to my sons with desperate strength,
Till the murderers loosed my hold at length,
And bore me breathless and faint aside,
In their iron arms, while my children died.
They died—and the mother that gave them
  birth
Is forbid to cover their bones with earth.

" The barley-harvest was nodding white,
When my children died on the rocky height,
And the reapers were singing on hill and plain,
When I came to my task of sorrow and pain.
But now the season of rain is nigh,
The sun is dim in the thickening sky,
And the clouds in the sullen darkness rest
Where he hides his light at the doors of the
  west.
I hear the howl of the wind that brings
The long drear storm on its heavy wings;
But the howling wind, and the driving rain
Will beat on my houseless head in vain :
I shall stay, from my murdered sons to scare
The beasts of the desert and fowls of air."

THE ARCTIC LOVER.

GONE is the long, long winter night,
  Look, my beloved one!
How glorious, through his depths of light,
  Rolls the majestic sun.
The willows, waked from winter's death,
Give out a fragrance like thy breath—
  The summer is begun!

Ay, 'tis the long bright summer day:
  Hark, to that mighty crash!
The loosened ice-ridge breaks away—
  The smitten waters flash.
Seaward the glittering mountain rides,
While, down its green translucent sides,
  The foamy torrents dash.

See, love, my boat is moored for thee,
  By ocean's weedy floor—
The petrel does not skim the sea
  More swiftly than my oar.
We'll go where, on the rocky isles,
Her eggs the screaming sea-fowl piles
  Beside the pebbly shore.

Or, bide thou where the poppy blows,
  With wind-flowers frail and fair,

While I, upon his isle of snows,
  Seek and defy the bear.
Fierce though he be, and huge of frame,
This arm his savage strength shall tame,
  And drag him from his lair.

When crimson sky and flamy cloud
  Bespeak the summer o'er,
And the dead valleys wear a shroud
  Of snows that melt no more,
I'll build of ice thy winter home,
With glistening walls and glassy dome,
  And spread with skins the floor.

The white fox by thy couch shall play;
  And, from the frozen skies,
The meteors of a mimic day
  Shall flash upon thine eyes.
And I—for such thy vow—meanwhile
Shall hear thy voice and see thy smile,
  Till that long midnight flies.

5   C

ROMERO.

WHEN freedom, from the land of Spain,
  By Spain's degenerate sons was driven,
Who gave their willing limbs again
  To wear the chain so lately riven;
Romero broke the sword he wore—
  "Go, faithful brand," the warrior said,
"Go, undishonored, never more
  The blood of man shall make thee **red;**
  I grieve for that already shed;
And I am sick at heart to know,
That faithful friend and noble foe
Have only bled to make more strong
The yoke that Spain has worn so long.
Wear it who will, in abject fear—
  I wear it not who have been free;
The perjured Ferdinand shall hear
  No oath of loyalty from me."
Then, hunted by the hounds of power,
  Romero chose a safe retreat,
Where bleak Nevada's summits tower
  Above the beauty at their feet.
    There once, when on his cabin lay
    The crimson light of setting day,
    When even on the mountain's breast
    The chainless winds were all at rest,
    And he could hear the river's flow

From the calm paradise below;
Warmed with his former fires again,
He framed this rude but solemn strain.

" Here will I make my home—for here at
least I see,
Upon this wild Sierra's side, the steps of Lib-
erty;
Where the locust chirps unscared beneath the
unpruned lime,
And the merry bee doth hide from man the
spoil of the mountain thyme;
Where the pure winds come and go, and the
wild vine strays at will,
An outcast from the haunts of men, she dwells
with Nature still.

" I see the valleys, Spain ! where thy mighty
rivers run,
And the hills that lift thy harvests and vine-
yards to the sun,
And the flocks that drink thy brooks and
sprinkle all the green,
Where lie thy plains, with sheep-walks seamed,
and olive shades between :
I see thy fig-trees bask, with the fair pome-
granate near,

And the fragrance of thy lemon-groves can
    almost reach me here.

  "Fair—fair—but fallen Spain! 'tis with a
    swelling heart,
That I think on all thou might'st have been,
    and look at what thou art;
But the strife is over now—and all the good
    and brave,
That would have raised thee up, are gone, to
    exile or the grave.
Thy fleeces are for monks, thy grapes for the
    convent feast,
And the wealth of all thy harvest-fields for the
    pampered lord and priest.

  "But I shall see the day—it will come before
    I die—
I shall see it in my silver hairs, and with an
    age-dimmed eye;—
When the spirit of the land to liberty shall
    bound,
As yonder fountain leaps away from the dark-
    ness of the ground;
And, to my mountain cell, the voices of the
    free
Shall rise, as from the beaten shore the thun-
    ders of the sea."

MONUMENT MOUNTAIN.

THOU who wouldst see the lovely and the wild
Mingled in harmony on Nature's face,
Ascend our rocky mountains. Let thy foot
Fail not with weariness, for on their tops
The beauty and the majesty of earth,
Spread wide beneath, shall make thee to forget
The steep and toilsome way. There, as thou
     stand'st,
The haunts of men below thee, and around
The mountain summits, thy expanding heart
Shall feel a kindred with that loftier world
To which thou art translated, and partake
The enlargement of thy vision.   Thou shalt
     look
Upon the green and rolling forest tops,
And down into the secrets of the glens,
And streams, that with their bordering thickets
     strive
To hide their windings. Thou shalt gaze, at
     once,
Here on white villages, and tilth, and herds,
And swarming roads, and there on solitudes
That only hear the torrent, and the wind,
And eagle's shriek.   There is a precipice
That seems a fragment of some mighty wall,
Built by the hand that fashioned the old world,

To separate its nations, and thrown down
When the flood drowned them.   To the north
    a path
Conducts you up the narrow battlement.
Steep is the western side, shaggy and wild
With mossy trees, and pinnacles of flint,
And many a hanging crag.   But, to the east,
Sheer to the vale go down the bare old cliffs,
Huge pillars, that in middle heaven upbear
Their weather-beaten capitals, here dark
With the thick moss of centuries, and there
Of chalky whiteness where the thunderbolt
Has splintered them.   It is a fearful thing
To stand upon the beetling verge, and see
Where storm and lightning, from that huge
    wall,
Have tumbled down vast blocks, and at the
    base
Dashed them in fragments, and to lay thine ear
Over the dizzy depth, and hear the sound
Of winds, that struggle with the woods below,
Come up like ocean murmurs.   But the scene
Is lovely round ; a beautiful river there
Wanders amid the fresh and fertile meads,
The paradise he made unto himself.
Mining the soil for ages.   On each side
The fields swell upward to the hills ; beyond,

Above the hills, in the blue distance, rise
The mighty columns with which earth props
    heaven.

    There is a tale about these gray old rocks,
A sad tradition of unhappy love
And sorrows borne and ended, long ago,
When over these fair vales the savage sought
His game in the thick woods. There was a
    maid,
The fairest of the Indian maids, bright-eyed,
With wealth of raven tresses, a light form,
And a gay heart. About her cabin door
The wide old woods resounded with her song
And fairy laughter all the summer day.
She loved her cousin ; such a love was deemed,
By the morality of those stern tribes,
Incestuous, and she struggled hard and long
Against her love, and reasoned with her heart,
As simple Indian maiden might. In vain.
Then her eye lost its lustre, and her step
Its lightness, and the gray old men that passed
Her dwelling, wondered that they heard no more
The accustomed song and laugh of her, whose
    looks
Were like the cheerful smile of Spring, they
    said,

Upon the Winter of their age.   She went
To weep where no eye saw, and was not found
When all the merry girls were met to dance,
And all the hunters of the tribe were out;
Nor when they gathered from the rustling husk
The shining ear; nor when, by the river's side,
They pulled the grape and startled the wild
        shades
With sounds of mirth.   The keen-eyed Indian
        dames
Would whisper to each other, as they saw
Her wasting form, and say, *the girl will die.*
    One day into the bosom of a friend,
A playmate of her young and innocent years,
She poured her griefs.   "Thou know'st, and
        thou alone,"
She said, "for I have told thee, all my love,
And guilt, and sorrow.   I am sick of life.
All night I weep in darkness, and the morn
Glares on me, as upon a thing accursed,
That has no business on the earth.   I hate
The pastimes and the pleasant toils that once
I loved; the cheerful voices of my friends
Have an unnatural horror in mine ear.
In dreams my mother, from the land of souls,
Calls me and chides me.   All that look on me
Do seem to know my shame; I cannot bear

Their eyes; I cannot from my heart root out
The love that wrings it so, and I must die."

It was a summer morning, and they went
To this old precipice.   About the cliffs
Lay garlands, ears of maize, and shaggy skins
Of wolf and bear, the offerings of the tribe
Here made to the Great Spirit, for they deemed,
Like worshippers of the elder time, that God
Doth walk on the high places and affect
The earth-o'erlooking mountains.   She had on
The ornaments with which her father loved
To deck the beauty of his bright-eyed girl,
And bade her wear when stranger warriors
      came
To be his guests.   Here the friends sat them
      down,
And sang, all day, old songs of love and death,
And decked the poor wan victim's hair with
      flowers,
And prayed that safe and swift might be her
      way
To the calm world of sunshine, where no grief
Makes the heart heavy and the eyelids red.
Beautiful lay the region of her tribe
Below her—waters resting in the embrace
Of the wide forest, and maize-planted glades

Opening amid the leafy wilderness.
She gazed upon it long, and at the sight
Of her own village peeping through the trees,
And her own dwelling, and the cabin roof
Of him she loved with an unlawful love,
And came to die for, a warm gush of tears
Ran from her eyes.   But when the sun grew
    low
And the hill shadows long, she threw herself
From the steep rock and perished.   There was
    scooped,
Upon the mountain's southern slope, a grave;
And there they laid her, in the very garb
With which the maiden decked herself for
    death
With the same withering wild flowers in her
    hair.
And o'er the mould that covered her, the tribe
Built up a simple monument, a cone
Of small loose stones.   Thenceforward, all
    who passed,
Hunter, and dame, and virgin, laid a stone
In silence on the pile.   It stands there yet.
And Indians from the distant West, who come
To visit where their fathers' bones are laid,
Yet tell the sorrowful tale, and to this day
The mountain where the hapless maiden died
Is called the Mountain of the Monument.

SONG OF MARION'S MEN.

OUR band is few, but true and tried,
  Our leader frank and bold;
The British soldier trembles
  When Marion's name is told.
Our fortress is the good greenwood,
  Our tent the cypress-tree;
We know the forest round us,
  As seamen know the sea.
We know its walls of thorny vines,
  Its glades of reedy grass,
Its safe and silent islands
  Within the dark morass.

Woe to the English soldiery
  That little dread us near!
On them shall light at midnight
  A strange and sudden fear:
When waking to their tents on fire
  They grasp their arms in vain,
And they who stand to face us
  Are beat to earth again;
And they who fly in terror deem
  A mighty host behind,
And hear the tramp of thousands
  Upon the hollow wind.

Then sweet the hour that brings release
   From danger and from toil:
We talk the battle over,
   And share the battle's spoil.
The woodland rings with laugh and shout,
   As if a hunt were up,
And woodland flowers are gathered
   To crown the soldier's cup.
With merry songs we mock the wind
   That in the pine-top grieves,
And slumber long and sweetly,
   On beds of oaken leaves.

Well knows the fair and friendly moon
   The band that Marion leads—
The glitter of their rifles,
   The scampering of their steeds.
'Tis life our fiery barbs to guide
   Across the moonlight plains;
'Tis life to feel the night-wind
   That lifts their tossing manes.
A moment in the British camp—
   A moment—and away
Back to the pathless forest,
   Before the peep of day.

Grave men there are by broad Santee,
   Grave men with hoary hairs,

Their hearts are all with Marion,
   For Marion are their prayers.
And lovely ladies greet our band,
   With kindliest welcoming,
With smiles like those of summer,
   And tears like those of spring.
For them we wear these trusty arms,
   And lay them down no more
Till we have driven the Briton,
   Forever from our shore.

THE DISINTERRED WARRIOR.

GATHER him to his grave again
   And solemnly and softly lay,
Beneath the verdure of the plain,
   The warrior's scattered bones away.
Pay the deep reverence, taught of old,
   The homage of man's heart to death;
Nor dare to trifle with the mould
   Once hallowed by the Almighty's breath.

The soul hath quickened every part—
   That remnant of a martial brow,
Those ribs that held the mighty heart,
   That strong arm—strong no longer now.

Spare them, each mouldering relic spare,
   Of God's own image ; let them rest,
Till not a trace shall speak of where
The awful likeness was impressed.

For he was fresher from the hand
   That formed of earth the human face,
And to the elements did stand
   In nearer kindred than our race.
In many a flood to madness tossed,
   In many a storm has been his path ;
He hid him not from heat or frost,
   But met them, and defied their wrath.

Then they were kind—the forests here,
   Rivers, and stiller waters paid
A tribute to the net and spear
   Of the red ruler of the shade.
Fruits on the woodland branches lay,
   Roots in the shaded soil below,
The stars looked forth to teach his way,
   The still earth warned him of the foe.

A noble race ! but they are gone,
   With their old forests wide and deep,
And we have built our homes upon
   Fields where their generations sleep.

Their fountains slake our thirst at noon,
　Upon their fields our harvest waves,
Our lovers woo beneath their moon—
　Ah, let us spare, at least, their graves!

THE HURRICANE.

LORD of the winds! I feel thee nigh,
I know thy breath in the burning sky!
And I wait, with a thrill in every vein,
For the coming of the hurricane!
　And lo! on the wing of the heavy gales,
Through the boundless arch of heaven he
　　sails; .
Silent, and slow, and terribly strong,
The mighty shadow is borne along,
Like the dark eternity to come;
While the world below, dismayed and dumb,
Through the calm of the thick hot atmosphere
Looks up at its gloomy folds with fear.
　They darken fast—and the golden blaze
Of the sun is quenched in the lurid·haze,
And he sends through the shade a funeral
　　ray—
A glare that is neither night nor day,
A beam that touches, with hues of death,

The clouds above and the earth beneath.
To its covert glides the silent bird,
While the hurricane's distant voice is heard,
Uplifted among the mountains round,
And the forests hear and answer the sound.

  He is come! he is come! do ye not behold
His ample robes on the wind unrolled?
Giant of air! we bid thee hail!—
How his gray skirts toss in the whirling gale;
How his huge and writhing arms are bent,
To clasp the zone of the firmament,
And fold, at length, in their dark embrace,
From mountain to mountain the visible space.

  Darker—still darker! the whirlwinds bear
The dust of the plains to the middle air:
And hark to the crashing, long and loud,
Of the chariot of God in the thunder-cloud!
You may trace its path by the flashes that start
From the rapid wheels where'er they dart,
As the fire-bolts leap to the world below,
And flood the skies with a lurid glow.

  What roar is that?—'tis the rain that breaks
In torrents away from the airy lakes,
Heavily poured on the shuddering ground,
And shedding a nameless horror round.
Ah! well-known woods. and mountains, and
    skies,

With the very clouds!—ye are lost to my eyes..
I seek ye vainly, and see in your place
The shadowy tempest that sweeps through
    space,
A whirling ocean that fills the wall
Of the crystal heaven and buries all.
And I, cut off from the world, remain
Alone with the terrible hurricane.

"OH FAIREST OF THE RURAL MAIDS."

OH fairest of the rural maids !
Thy birth was in the forest shades ;
Green boughs, and glimpses of the sky,
Were all that met thy infant eye.

Thy sports, thy wanderings, when a child,
Were ever in the sylvan wild ;
And all the beauty of the place,
Is in thy heart and on thy face.

The twilight of the trees and rocks
Is in the light shade of thy locks ;
Thy step is as the wind, that weaves
Its playful way among the leaves.

6

Thy eyes are springs, in whose serene
And silent waters heaven is seen ;
Their lashes are the herbs that look
On their young figures in the brook.

The forest depths, by foot unpressed,
Are not more sinless than thy breast ;
The holy peace that fills the air
Of those calm solitudes is there.

INSCRIPTION FOR THE ENTRANCE TO A WOOD.

STRANGER, if thou hast learned a truth
    which needs
No school of long experience, that the world
Is full of guilt and misery, and has seen
Enough of all its sorrows, crimes, and cares,
To tire thee of it, enter this wild wood
And view the haunts of Nature. The calm
    shade
Shall bring a kindred calm, and the sweet
    breeze
That makes the green leaves dance, shall waft
    a balm
To thy sick heart. Thou wilt find nothing here
Of all that pained thee in the haunts of men

And made thee loathe thy life. The primal
    curse
Fell, it is true, upon the unsinning earth,
But not in vengeance. God hath yoked to
    Guilt
Her pale tormentor, Misery. Hence these
    shades
Are still the abodes of gladness; the thick roof
Of green and stirring branches is alive
And musical with birds, that sing and sport
In wantonness of spirit; while below
The squirrel, with raised paws and form erect,
Chirps merrily. Throngs of insects in the
    shade
Try their thin wings and dance in the warm
    beam
That waked them into life. Even the green
    trees
Partake the deep contentment; as they bend
To the soft winds, the sun from the blue sky
Looks in and sheds a blessing on the scene.
Scarce less the cleft-born wild-flower seems to
    enjoy
Existence, than the winged plunderer
That sucks its sweets. The massy rocks them-
    selves,

And the old and ponderous trunks of prostrate
    trees
That lead from knoll to knoll a causey rude
Or bridge the sunken brook, and their dark
    roots,
With all their earth upon them, twisting high,
Breathed fixed tranquillity. The rivulet
Sends forth glad sounds, and tripping o'er its
    bed
Of pebbly sands, or leaping down the rocks,
Seems, with continuous laughter, to rejoice
In its own being. Softly tread the marge,
Lest from her midway perch thou scare the
    wren
That dips her bill in water. The cool wind,
That stirs the stream in play, shall come to
    thee,
Like one that loves thee nor will let thee pass
Ungreeted, and shall give its light embrace.

TO A MOSQUITO.

FAIR insect! that, with threadlike legs spread
    out,
  And blood-extracting bill and filmy wing,
Dost murmur, as thou slowly sail'st about,

In pitiless ears full many a plaintive thing,
And tell how little our large veins should bleed,
Would we but yield them to thy bitter need.

Unwillingly, I own, and, what is worse,
    Full angrily, men hearken to thy plaint,
Thou gettest many a brush, and many a curse,
    For saying thou art gaunt, and starved, and
        faint;
Even the old beggar, while he asks for food,
Would kill thee, hapless stranger, if he could.

I call thee stranger, for the town, I ween,
    Has not the honor of so proud a birth,
Thou com'st from Jersey meadows, fresh and
        green,
    The offspring of the gods, though born on
        earth;
For Titan was thy sire, and fair was she,
The ocean nymph, that nursed thy infancy.

Beneath the rushes was thy cradle swung,
    And when, at length, thy gauzy wings grew
        strong,
Abroad to gentle airs their folds were flung,
    Rose in the sky and bore thee soft along:
The south wind breathed to waft thee on thy
        way,

And danced and shone beneath the billowy
   bay.

And calm, afar, the city spires arose,—
   Thence didst thou hear the distant hum of
    men,
And as its grateful odors met thy nose,
   Didst seem to smell thy native marsh again;
Fair lay its crowded streets, and at the sight
Thy tiny songs grew shriller with delight.

At length thy pinions fluttered in Broadway—
   Ah, there were fairy steps, and white necks
    kissed
By wanton airs, and eyes whose killing ray
   Shone through the snowy veils like stars
    through mist;
And fresh as morn, on many a cheek and chin,
Bloomed the bright blood through the trans-
    parent skin.

Oh, these were sights to touch an anchorite!
   What! do I hear thy slender voice complain?
Thou wailest, when I talk of beauty's light,
   As if it brought the memory of pain:
Thou art a wayward being—well—come near,
And pour thy tale of sorrow in my ear.

What say'st thou—slanderer!—rouge makes
    thee sick?
And China bloom at best is sorry food?
And Rowland's Kalydor, if laid on thick,
    Poisons the thirsty wretch that bores for
    blood?
Go! 'twas a just reward that met thy crime—
But shun the sacrilege another time.

That bloom was made to look at, not to touch,
    To worship, not approach, that radiant white;
And well might sudden vengeance light on such
    As dared, like thee, most impiously to bite.
Thou shouldst have gazed at distance and ad-
    mired,
Murmured thy adoration and retired.

Thou'rt welcome to the town—but why come
    here
    To bleed a brother poet, gaunt like thee?
Alas! the little blood I have is dear,
    And thin will be the banquet drawn from me.
Look round—the pale-eyed sisters in my cell,
Thy old acquaintance, Song and Famine, dwell.

Try some plump alderman, and suck the blood
    Enriched by generous wine and costly meat;

On well-filled skins, sleek as thy native mud,
  Fix thy light pump and press thy freckled
    feet:
Go to the men for whom, in ocean's halls,
The oyster breeds, and the green turtle sprawls.

There corks are drawn, and the red vintage
  flows
  To fill the swelling veins for thee, and now
The ruddy cheek and now the ruddier nose
  Shall tempt thee, as thou flittest round the
    brow;
And, when the hour of sleep its quiet brings,
No angry hand shall rise to brush thy wings.

"I BROKE THE SPELL THAT HELD ME LONG."

I BROKE the spell that held me long,
The dear, dear witchery of song.
I said, the poet's idle lore
Shall waste my prime of years no more,
For Poetry, though heavenly born,
Consorts with poverty and scorn.

I broke the spell—nor deemed its power
Could fetter me another hour.

Ah, thoughtless! how could I forget
Its causes were around me yet?
For whereso'er I looked, the while,
Was Nature's everlasting smile.

Still came and lingered on my sight
Of flowers and streams the bloom and light,
And glory of the stars and sun;—
And these and poetry are one.
They, ere the world had held me long,
Recalled me to the love of song.

THE CONJUNCTION OF JUPITER AND VENUS.

I would not always reason. The straight
    path
Wearies us with its never-varying lines,
And we grow melancholy. I would make
Reason my guide, but she should sometimes sit
Patiently by the way-side, while I traced
The mazes of the pleasant wilderness
Around me. She should be my counsellor,
But not my tyrant. For the spirit needs
Impulses from a deeper source than hers,
And there are motions, in the mind of man,
That she must look upon with awe. I bow

Reverently to her dictates, but not less
Hold to the fair illusions of old time—
lllusions that shed brightness over life,
And glory over nature.   Look, even now,
Where two bright planets in the twilight meet,
Upon the saffron heaven,—the imperial star
Of Jove, and she that from her radiant urn
Pours forth the light of love.   Let me believe,
Awhile, that they are met for ends of good,
Amid the evening glory, to confer
Of men and their affairs, and to shed down
Kind influence.   Lo! their orbs burn more
        bright,
And shake out softer fires! The great earth
        feels
The gladness and the quiet of the time.
Meekly the mighty river, that infolds
This mighty city, smooths his front, and far
Glitters and burns even to the rocky base
Of the dark heights that bound him to the
        West;
And a deep murmur, from the many streets,
Rises like a thanksgiving.   Put we hence
Dark and sad thoughts awhile—there's time
        for them
Hereafter—on the morrow we will meet,
With melancholy looks, to tell our griefs,

And make each other wretched; this calm
    hour,
This balmy, blessed evening, we will give
To cheerful hopes and dreams of happy days,
Born of the meeting of those glorious stars.

    Enough of drought has parched the year,
    and scared
The land with dread of famine. Autumn, yet,
Shall make men glad with unexpected fruits.
The dog-star shall shine harmless; genial days
Shall softly glide away into the keen
And wholesome cold of winter; he that fears
The pestilence, shall gaze on those pure beams,
And breathe, with confidence, the quiet air.

    Emblems of power and beauty! well may
    they
Shine brightest on our borders, and withdraw
Toward the great Pacific, marking out
The path of empire. Thus, in our own land,
Erelong, the better Genius of our race,
Having encompassed earth, and tamed its
    tribes,
Shall sit him down beneath the farthest West,
By the shore of that calm ocean, and look back
On realms made happy.

Light the nuptial torch,
And say the glad, yet solemn rite, that knits
The youth and maiden.   Happy days to them
That wed this evening !—a long life of love,
And blooming sons and daughters !   Happy
    they
Born at this hour,—for they shall see an age
Whiter and holier than the past, and go
Late to their graves.   Men shall wear softer
    hearts,
And shudder at the butcheries of war,
As now at other murders.

Hapless Greece !
Enough of blood has wet thy rocks, and
    stained
Thy rivers ; deep enough thy chains have worn
Their links into thy flesh; the sacrifice
Of thy pure maidens, and thy innocent babes,
And reverend priests, has expiated all
Thy crimes of old.   In yonder mingling lights
There is an omen of good days for thee.
Thou shalt arise from 'midst the dust and sit
Again among the nations.   Thine own arm
Shall yet redeem thee.   Not in wars like thine
The world takes part.   Be it a strife of kings,—
Despot with despot battling for a throne,—

And Europe shall be stirred throughout her
    realms,
Nations shall put on harness, and shall fall
Upon each other, and in all their bounds
The wailing of the childless shall not cease.
Thine is a war for liberty, and thou
Must fight it single-handed.   The old world
Looks coldly on the murderers of thy race,
And leaves thee to the struggle ; and the new,—
I fear me thou couldst tell a shameful tale
Of fraud and lust of gain ;—thy treasury
    drained,
And Missolonghi fallen.   Yet thy wrongs
Shall put new strength into thy heart and hand,
And God and thy good sword shall yet work
    out,
For thee, a terrible deliverance.

TO THE FRINGED GENTIAN.

Thou blossom bright with autumn dew,
And colored with the heaven's own blue,
That openest, when the quiet light
Succeeds the keen and frosty night.

Thou comest not when violets lean
O'er wandering brooks and springs unseen,

Or columbines, in purple dressed,
Nod o'er the ground-bird's hidden nest.

Thou waitest late, and com'st alone,
When woods are bare and birds are flown,
And frosts and shortening days portend
The aged year is near his end.

Then doth thy sweet and quiet eye
Look through its fringes to the sky,
Blue—blue—as if that sky let fall
A flower from its cerulean wall.

I would that thus, when I shall see
The hour of death draw near to me,
Hope, blossoming within my heart,
May look to heaven as I depart.

"INNOCENT CHILD AND SNOW-WHITE FLOWER."

Innocent child and snow-white flower!
Well are ye paired in your opening hour.
Thus should the pure and the lovely meet,
Stainless with stainless, and sweet with sweet.

White as those leaves, just blown apart,
Are the folds of thy own young heart;
Guilty passion and cankering care
Never have left their traces there.

Artless one! though thou gazest now
O'er the white blossom with earnest brow,
Soon will it tire thy childish eye,
Fair as it is, thou wilt throw it by.

Throw it aside in thy weary hour,
Throw to the ground the fair white flower,
Yet, as thy tender years depart,
Keep that white and innocent heart.

AN INDIAN AT THE BURIAL-PLACE
OF HIS FATHERS.

IT is the spot I came to seek,—
  My fathers' ancient burial-place,
Ere from these vales, ashamed and weak,
  Withdrew our wasted race.
It is the spot,—I know it well—
Of which our old traditions tell.

For here the upland bank sends out
   A ridge toward the river-side;
I know the shaggy hills about,
   The meadows smooth and wide,
The plains, that, toward the southern sky,
Fenced east and west by mountains lie.

A white man, gazing on the scene,
   Would say a lovely spot was here,
And praise the lawns, so fresh and green,
   Between the hills so sheer.
I like it not—I would the plain
Lay in its tall old groves again.

The sheep are on the slopes around,
   The cattle in the meadows feed,
And laborers turn the crumbling ground,
   Or drop the yellow seed,
And prancing steeds, in trappings gay,
Whirl the bright chariot o'er the way.

Methinks it were a nobler sight
   To see these vales in woods arrayed,
Their summits in the golden light,
   Their trunks in grateful shade,
And herds of deer, that bounding go
O'er rills and prostrate trees below.

And then to mark the lord of all,
   The forest hero, trained to wars,
Quivered and plumed, and lithe and tall,
   And seamed with glorious scars,
Walk forth, amid his reign, to dare
The wolf, and grapple with the bear.

This bank, in which the dead were laid,
   Was sacred when its soil was ours;
Hither the artless Indian maid
   Brought wreaths of beads and flowers,
And the gray chief and gifted seer
Worshipped the god of thunders here.

But now the wheat is green and high
   On clods that hid the warrior's breast,
And scattered in the furrows lie
   The weapons of his rest,
And there, in the loose sand, is thrown
Of his large arm the mouldering bone.

Ah, little thought the strong and brave,
   Who bore the lifeless chieftain forth;
Or the young wife, that weeping gave
   Her first born to the earth,
That the pale race, who waste us now,
Among their bones should guide the plough.

They waste us—ay—like April snow
  In the warm noon, we shrink away;
And fast they follow, as we go
  Towards the setting day,—
Till they shall fill the land, and we
Are driven into the western sea.

But I behold a fearful sign,
  To which the white men's eyes are blind;
Their race may vanish hence, like mine.
  And leave no trace behind,
Save ruins o'er the region spread,
And the white stones above the dead.

Before these fields were shorn and tilled,
  Full to the brim our rivers flowed;
The melody of waters filled
  The fresh and boundless wood;
And torrents dashed and rivulets played,
And fountains spouted in the shade.

Those grateful sounds are heard no more,
  The springs are silent in the sun,
The rivers, by the blackened shore,
  With lessening current run;
The realm our tribes are crushed to get
May be a barren desert yet.

TO A CLOUD.

BEAUTIFUL cloud! with folds so soft and fair,
Swimming in the pure quiet air!
Thy fleeces bathed in sunlight, while below
Thy shadow o'er the vale moves slow;
Where, midst their labor, pause the reaper
    train
As cool it comes along the grain.
Beautiful cloud! I would I were with thee
In thy calm way o'er land and sea:
To rest on thy unrolling skirts, and look
On Earth as on an open book;
On streams that tie her realms with silver bands,
And the long ways that seam her lands;
And hear her humming cities, and the sound
Of the great ocean breaking round.
Ay—I would sail upon thy air-borne car
To blooming regions distant far,
To where the sun of Andalusia shines
On his own olive-groves and vines,
Or the soft lights of Italy's bright sky
In smiles upon her ruins lie.
But I would woo the winds to let us rest
O'er Greece long fettered and oppressed,
Whose sons at length have heard the call that
    comes
From the old battle-fields and tombs,

And risen, and drawn the sword, and on the foe
Have dealt the swift and desperate blow,
And the Othman power is cloven, and the
    stroke
Has touched its chains, and they are broke.
Ay, we would linger till the sunset there
Should come, to purple all the air,
And thou reflect upon the sacred ground
The ruddy radiance streaming round.

Bright meteor ! for the summer noontide made !
Thy peerless beauty yet shall fade.
The sun, that fills with light each glistening
    fold,
Shall set, and leave thee dark and cold :
The blast shall rend thy skirts, or thou may'st
    frown .
In the dark heaven when storms come down,
And weep in rain, till man's inquiring eye
Miss thee, forever, from the sky.

THE YELLOW VIOLET.

When beechen buds begin to swell,
  And woods the blue-bird's warble know,
The yellow violet's modest bell
  Peeps from the last year's leaves below.

Ere russet fields their green resume,
  Sweet flower, I love, in forest bare,
To meet thee, when thy faint perfume
  Alone is in the virgin air.

Of all her train, the hands of Spring
  First plant thee in the watery mould,
And I have seen thee blossoming
  Beside the snow-bank's edges cold.

Thy parent sun, who bade thee view,
  Pale skies, and chilling moisture sip,
Has bathed thee in his own bright hue,
  And streaked with jet thy glowing lip.

Yet slight thy form, and low thy seat,
  And earthward bent thy gentle eye,
Unapt the passing view to meet,
  When loftier flowers are flaunting nigh.

Oft, in the sunless April day,
  Thy early smile has stayed my walk,
But, 'midst the gorgeous blooms of May,
  I passed thee on thy humble stalk.

So they, who climb to wealth, forget
  The friends in darker fortunes tried
I copied them—but I regret
  That I should ape the ways of pride.

And when again the genial hour
  Awakes the painted tribes of light,
I'll not o'erlook the modest flower
  That made the woods of April bright.

"I CANNOT FORGET WITH WHAT FERVID DEVOTION."

I CANNOT forget with what fervid devotion
  I worshipped the visions of verse and of
    fame;
Each gaze at the glories of earth, sky, and
    ocean,
  To my kindled emotions, was wind over
    flame.

And deep were my musings in life's early
    blossom,
  'Mid the twilight of mountain groves wan-
    dering long;
How thrilled my young veins, and how throbbed
    my full bosom,
  When o'er me descended the spirit of song.

'Mong the deep-cloven fells that for ages had
    listened
    To the rush of the pebble-paved river be-
        tween,
Where the kingfisher screamed and gray pre-
    cipice glistened,
    All breathless with awe have I gazed on the
        scene ;

Till I felt the dark power o'er my reveries
    stealing,
    From his throne in the depth of that stern
        solitude,
And he breathed through my lips, in that
    tempest of feeling,
    Strains warm with his spirit, though artless
        and rude.

Bright visions ! I mixed with the world and ye
    faded ;
    No longer your pure rural worshipper now ;
In the haunts your continual presence pervaded,
    Ye shrink from the signet of care on my brow.

In the old mossy groves on the breast of the
    mountain,
    In deep lonely glens where the waters com-
        plain,

By the shade of the rock, by the gush of the
    fountain,
  I seek your loved footsteps, but seek them in
    vain.

Oh, leave not. forlorn and forever forsaken,
  Your pupil and victim, to life and its tears !
But sometimes return, and in mercy awaken
  The glories ye showed to his earlier years.

MUTATION.

(A SONNET.)

THEY talk of short-lived pleasure—be it so—
  Pain dies as quickly: stern, hard-featured
    pain
Expires, and lets her weary prisoner go.
  The fiercest agonies have shortest reign ;
  And after dreams of horror, comes again
The welcome morning with its rays of peace.
  Oblivion, softly wiping out the stain,
Makes the strong secret pangs of shame to
    cease :
Remorse is virtue's root ; its fair increase
  Are fruits of innocence and blessedness :

Thus joy, o'erborne and bound, doth still re-
    lease .
  His young limbs from the chains that round
    him press.
Weep not that the world changes—did it keep
A stable changeless state, 'twere cause indeed
    to weep.

HYMN TO THE NORTH STAR.

  THE sad and solemn night
Has yet her multitude of cheerful fires ;
  The glorious host of light
Walk the dark hemisphere till she retires ;
All through her silent watches, gliding slow,
Her constellations come, and climb the heavens,
    and go.

  Day, too, hath many a star
To grace his gorgeous reign, as bright as they :
  Through the blue fields afar,
Unseen, they follow in his flaming way :
Many a bright lingerer, as the eve grows dim,
Tells what a radiant troop arose and set with
    him.

And thou dost see them rise,
Star of the Pole! and thou dost see them set.
    Alone, in thy cold skies,
Thou keep'st thy old unmoving station yet,
Nor join'st the dances of that glittering train,
Nor dipp'st thy virgin orb in the blue western
    main.

    There, at morn's rosy birth,
Thou lookest meekly through the kindling air,
    And eve, that round the earth
Chases the day, beholds thee watching there;
There noontide finds thee, and the hour that
    calls
The shapes of polar flame to scale heaven's
    azure walls.

    Alike, beneath thine eye,
The deeds of darkness and of light are done;
    High toward the star-lit sky
Towns blaze—the smoke of battle blots the
    sun—
The night-storm on a thousand hills is loud—
And the strong wind of day doth mingle sea
    and cloud.

On thy unaltering blaze
The half-wrecked mariner, his compass lost,
  Fixes his steady gaze,
And steers, undoubting, to the friendly coast;
And they who stray in perilous wastes, by
    night,
Are glad when thou dost shine to guide their
    footsteps right.

And, therefore, bards of old,
Sages, and hermits of the solemn wood,
  Did in thy beams behold
A beauteous type of that unchanging good,
That bright eternal beacon, by whose ray
The voyager of time should shape his heedful
    way.

THE TWENTY-SECOND OF DECEMBER.

WILD was the day; the wintry sea
  Moaned sadly on New England's strand,
When first, the thoughtful and the free,
  Our fathers trod the desert land.

They little thought how pure a light,
  With years, should gather round that day;

How love should keep their memories bright,
How wide a realm their sons should sway.

Green are their bays; but greener still
Shall round their spreading fame be wreathed,
And regions, now untrod, shall thrill
With reverence, when their names are
breathed.

Till where the sun, with softer fires,
Looks on the vast Pacific's sleep,
The children of the pilgrim sires
This hallowed day like us shall keep.

HYMN OF THE WALDENSES.

HEAR, Father, hear thy faint afflicted flock
Cry to thee, from the desert and the rock;
While those, who seek to slay thy children,
hold
Blasphemous worship under roofs of gold;
And the broad goodly lands, with pleasant airs
That nurse the grape and wave the grain, are
theirs.

Yet better were this mountain wilderness,
And this wild life of danger and distress—
Watchings by night and perilous flight by day,
And meetings in the depths of earth to pray,
Better, far better, than to kneel with them,
And pay the impious rite thy laws condemn.

Thou, Lord, dost hold the thunder; the firm
    land
Tosses in billows when it feels thy hand ;
Thou dashest nation against nation, then
Stillest the angry world to peace again.
Oh, touch their stony hearts who hunt thy sons—
The murderers of our wives and little ones.

Yet, mighty God, yet shall thy frown look forth
Unveiled, and terribly shall shake the earth.
Then the foul power of priestly sin and all
Its long-upheld idolatries shall fall.
Thou shalt raise up the trampled and oppressed,
And thy delivered saints shall dwell in rest.

SONG OF THE STARS.

WHEN the radiant morn of creation broke,
And the world in the smile of God awoke,
And the empty realms of darkness and death
Were moved through their depths by his mighty
    breath,
And orbs of beauty and spheres of flame
From the void abyss by myriads came, —
In the joy of youth as they darted away,
Through the widening wastes of space to play,
Their silver voices in chorus rung,
And this was the song the bright ones sung.

" Away, away, through the wide, wide sky, —
The fair blue fields that before us lie, —
Each sun, with the worlds that round him roll,
Each planet, poised on her turning pole;
With her isles of green and her clouds of
    white,
And her waters that lie like fluid light.

" For the source of glory uncovers his face,
And the brightness o'erflows unbounded space
And we drink, as we go, the luminous tides
In our ruddy air and our blooming sides :
Lo, yonder the living splendors play·
Away, on our joyous path, away !

" Look, look, through our glittering ranks afar,
In the infinite azure, star after star,
How they brighten and bloom as they swiftly
    pass !
How the verdure runs o'er each rolling mass !
And the path of the gentle winds is seen,
Where the small waves dance, and the young
    woods lean.

" And see, where the brighter day-beams pour,
How the rainbows hang in the sunny shower ;
And the morn and eve, with their pomp of hues,
Shift o'er the bright planets and shed their
    dews ;
And 'twixt them both, o'er the teeming ground,
With their shadowy cone the night goes round !

* Away, away ! in our blossoming bowers,
In the soft air wrapping these spheres of ours,
In the seas and fountains that shine with morn,
See, Love is brooding, and Life is born,
And breathing myriads are breaking from
    night,
To rejoice like us, in motion and light.

" Glide on in your beauty, ye youthful spheres,
To weave the dance that measures the years ;

Glide on, in the glory and gladness sent,
To the farthest wall of the firmament,—
The boundless visible smile of Him,
To the veil of whose brow your lamps are dim.

"NO MAN KNOWETH HIS SEPULCHRE."

WHEN he, who, from the scourge of wrong,
   Aroused the Hebrew tribes to fly,
Saw the fair region, promised long,
   And bowed him on the hills to die;

God made his grave, to men unknown,
   Where Moab's rocks a vale infold,
And laid the aged seer alone
   To slumber while the world grows old.

Thus still, whene'er the good and just
   Close the dim eye on life and pain,
Heaven watches o'er their sleeping dust,
   Till the pure spirit comes again.

Though nameless, trampled, and forgot,
   His servant's humble ashes lie,
Yet God has marked and sealed the spot,
   To call its inmates to the sky.

"BLESSED ARE THEY THAT MOURN."

OH, deem not they are blest alone
 Whose lives a peaceful tenor keep;
The Power who pities man, has shown
 A blessing for the eyes that weep.

The light of smiles shall fill again
 The lids that overflow with tears;
And weary hours of woe and pain
 Are promises of happier years.

There is a day of sunny rest
 For every dark and troubled night;
And grief may bide, an evening guest,
 But joy shall come with early light.

And thou, who, o'er thy friend's low bier
 Sheddest the bitter drops like rain,
Hope that a brighter, happier sphere,
 Will give him to thy arms again.

Nor let the good man's trust depart,
 Though life its common gifts deny,
Though with a pierced and bleeding heart,
 And spurned of men, he goes to die

8

For God has marked each sorrowing day,
  And numbered every secret tear,
And heaven's long age of bliss shall pay
  For all his children suffer here.

THE DEATH OF THE FLOWERS.

THE melancholy days are come, the saddest of
    the year,
Of wailing winds, and naked woods, and
    meadows brown and sear.
Heaped in the hollows of the grove, the with-
    ered leaves lie dead ;
They rustle to the eddying gust, and to the
    rabbit's tread.
The robin and the wren are flown, and from
    the shrubs the jay,
And from the wood-top calls the crow, through
    all the gloomy day.

Where are the flowers, the fair young flowers,
    that lately sprang and stood
In brighter light and softer air, a beauteous
    sisterhood ?

Alas! they all are in their graves, the gentle
    race of flowers
Are lying in their lowly beds, with the fair and
    good of ours.
The rain is falling where they lie, but the cold
    November rain,
Calls not, from out the gloomy earth, the lovely
    ones again.

The wind-flower and the violet, they perished
    long ago,
And the brier-rose and the orchis died amid the
    summer glow;
But on the hill the golden-rod, and the aster in
    the wood,
And the yellow sun-flower by the brook in
    autumn beauty stood,
Till fell the frost from the clear cold heaven, as
    falls the plague on men,
And the brightness of their smile was gone,
    from upland, glade, and glen.

And now, when comes the calm mild day, as
    still such days will come,
To call the squirrel and the bee from out their
    winter home;

When the sound of dropping nuts is heard,
  though all the trees are still,
And twinkle in the smoky light the waters of
  the rill,
The south wind searches for the flowers whose
  fragrance late he bore,
And sighs to find them in the wood and by the
  stream no more.

And then I think of one who in her youthful
  beauty died,
The fair, meek blossom that grew up and faded
  by my side;
In the cold moist earth we laid her, when the
  forest cast the leaf,
And we wept that one so lovely should have a
  life so brief:
Yet not unmeet it was that one, like that young
  friend of ours,
So gentle and so beautiful, should perish with
  the flowers.

TO A WATERFOWL.

WHITHER, 'midst falling dew,
While glow the heavens with the last steps of
    day,
Far, through their rosy depths, dost thou pursue
    Thy solitary way ?

    Vainly the fowler's eye
Might mark thy distant flight to do thee wrong,
As, darkly painted on the crimson sky,
    Thy figure floats along.

    Seek'st thou the plashy brink
Of weedy lake, or marge of river wide,
Or where the rocking billows rise and sink
    On the chafed ocean side ?

    There is a Power whose care
Teaches thy way along that pathless coast,
The desert and illimitable air—
    Lone wandering, but not lost.

    All day thy wings have fanned,
At that far height, the cold thin atmosphere,
Yet stoop not, weary, to the welcome land,
    Though the dark night is near,

And soon that toil shall end;
Soon shalt thou find a summer home, and rest,
And scream among thy fellows; reeds shall
    bend,
    Soon, o'er thy sheltered nest.

Thou'rt gone, the abyss of heaven
Hath swallowed up thy form; yet, on my heart
Deeply hath sunk the lesson thou hast given,
    And shall not soon depart.

He who, from zone to zone,
Guides through the boundless sky thy certain
    flight,
In the long way that I must tread alone
    Will lead my steps aright.

THE BATTLE-FIELD.

ONCE this soft turf, this rivulet's sands,
    Were trampled by a hurrying crowd,
And fiery hearts and armed hands
    Encountered in the battle cloud.

Ah! never shall the land forget
    How gushed the life-blood of her brave—

Gushed, warm with hope and valor yet,
    Upon the soil they fought to save.

Now all is calm and fresh and still,
    Alone the chirp of flitting bird,
And talk of children on the hill,
    And bell of wandering kine, are heard.

No solemn host goes trailing by
    The black-mouthed gun and staggering wain;
Men start not at the battle cry;
    Oh, be it never heard again!

Soon rested those who fought—but thou,
    Who minglest in the harder·strife
For truths which men receive not now,
    Thy warfare only ends with life.

A friendless warfare! lingering long
    Through weary day and weary year;
A wild and many-weaponed throng
    Hang on thy front and flank and rear.

Yet nerve thy spirit to the proof,
    And blench not at thy chosen lot;
The timid good may stand aloof,
    The sage may frown—yet faint thou not!

Nor heed the shaft too surely cast.
   The hissing, stinging bolt of scorn ·
For with thy side shall dwell, at last,
   The victory of endurance born.

Truth, crushed to earth, shall rise again;
   The eternal years of God are hers;
But Error, wounded, writhes with pain,
   And dies among his worshippers.

Yea, though thou lie upon the dust,
   When those who helped thee flee in fear,
Die full of hope and manly trust,
   Like those who fell in battle here.

Another hand thy sword shall wield,
   Another hand the standard wave,
Till from the trumpet's mouth is pealed
   The blast of triumph o'er thy grave!

THE WINDS.

YE winds, ye unseen currents of the air,
   Softly ye played a few brief hours ago;
Ye bore the murmuring bee; ye tossed the hair
   O'er maiden cheeks, that took a fresher glow;

Ye rolled the round white cloud through depths
    of blue ;
Ye shook from shaded flowers the lingering dew; —
Before you the catalpa's blossoms flew,
    Light blossoms, dropping on the grass like
    snow.

How are ye changed ! Ye take the cataract's
    sound ;
    Ye take the whirlpool's fury and its might;
The mountain shudders as ye sweep the ground ;
    The valley woods lie prone beneath your
    flight.
The clouds before you shoot like eagles past ;
The homes of men are rocking in your blast;
Ye lift the roofs like autumn leaves, and cast,
    Skyward, the whirling fragments out of sight.

The weary fowls of heaven make wing in vain,
    To 'scape your wrath ; ye seize and dash
    them dead.
Against the earth ye drive the roaring rain ;
    The harvest field becomes a river's bed ;
And torrents tumble from the hills around,
Plains turn to lakes, and villages are drowned,
And wailing voices, 'midst the tempest's sound,
    Rise, as the rushing waters swell and spread.

Ye dart upon the deep, and straight is heard
   A wilder roar, and men grow pale, and pray;
Ye fling its floods around you, as a bird
    Flings o'er his shivering plumes the fountain's
      spray.
See! to the breaking mast the sailor clings;
Ye scoop the ocean to its briny springs,
And take the mountain billow on your wings,
   And pile the wreck of navies round the bay.

Why rage ye thus?—no strife for liberty
   Has made you mad; no tyrant, strong
     through fear,
Has chained your pinions till ye wrenched
     them free,
   And rushed into the unmeasured atmosphere:
For ye were born in freedom where ye blow;
Free o'er the mighty deep to come and go;
Earth's solemn woods were yours, her wastes
     of snow,
   Her isles where summer blossoms all the year.

O ye wild winds, a mightier Power than yours
   In chains upon the shore of Europe lies;
The sceptered throng, whose fetters he endures,
   Watch his mute throes with terror in their
     eyes:

And armed warriors all around him stand,
And, as he struggles, tighten every band,
And lift the heavy spear, with threatening hand,
　To pierce the victim, should he strive to rise

Yet oh, when that wronged Spirit of our race
　Shall break, as soon he must, his long-worn
　　chains,
And leap in freedom from his prison-place,
　Lord of his ancient hills and fruitful plains,
Let him not rise, like these mad winds of air,
To waste the loveliness that time could spare,
To fill the earth with woe, and blot her fair
　Unconscious breast with blood from human
　　veins.

But may he like the Spring-time come abroad,
　Who crumbles winter's gyves with gentle
　　might,
When in the genial breeze, the breath of God,
Come spouting up the unsealed springs to light;
Flowers start from their dark prisons at his feet, —
The woods, long dumb, await to hymnings
　sweet,
And morn and eve, whose glimmerings almost
　meet,
　Crowd back to narrow bounds the ancient
　　night.

THE GREEN MOUNTAIN BOYS.

HERE we halt our march, and pitch our tent,
  On the rugged forest ground,
And light our fire with the branches rent,
  By winds from the beeches round.
Wild storms have torn this ancient wood,
  But a wilder is at hand,
With hail of iron and rain of blood,
  To sweep and scath the land.

How the bark waste rings with voices shrill,
  That startle the sleeping bird,
To-morrow eve must the voice be still,
  And the step must fall unheard.
The Briton lies by the blue Champlain,
  In Ticonderoga's towers,
And ere the sun rise twice again,
  The towers and the lake are ours.

Fill up the bowl from the brook that glides,
  Where the fireflies light the brake;
A ruddier juice the Briton hides,
  In his fortress by the lake.
Build high the fire, till the panther leap
  From his lofty perch in fright,
And we'll strengthen our weary arms with sleep,
  For the deeds of to-morrow night.

THE FUTURE LIFE.

How shall I know thee in the sphere which
    keeps
  The disembodied spirits of the dead,
When all of thee that time could wither sleeps
  And perishes among the dust we tread?

For I shall feel the sting of ceaseless pain
  If there I meet thy gentle presence not;
Nor hear the voice I love, nor read again
  In thy serenest eyes the tender thought.

Will not thy own meek heart demand me there?
  That heart whose fondest throbs to me were
    given?
My name on earth was ever in thy prayer,
  Shall it be banished from thy tongue in
    heaven?

In meadows fanned by heaven's life-breathing
    wind,
  In the resplendence of that glorious sphere,
And larger movements of the unfettered mind,
  Wilt thou forget the love that joined us here?

The love that lived through all the stormy past,
  And meekly with my harsher nature bore,
And deeper grew, and tenderer to the last,
  Shall it expire with life, and be no more?

A happier lot than mine, and larger light,
  Await thee there; for thou hast bowed thy
    will
In cheerful homage to the rule of right,
  And lovest all, and renderest good for ill.

For me, the sordid cares in which I dwell,
  Shrink and consume my heart, as heat the
    scroll;
And wrath hath left its scar—that fire of hell
  Has left its frightful scar upon my soul.

Yet, though thou wear'st the glory of the sky,
  Wilt thou not keep the same beloved name,
The same fair thoughtful brow, and gentle eye,
  Lovelier in heaven's sweet climate, yet the
    same?

Shalt thou not teach me, in that calmer home,
  The wisdom that I learned so ill in this—
The wisdom which is love—till I become
  Thy fit companion in that land of bliss?

THE OLD MAN'S COUNSEL.

AMONG our hills and valleys, I have known
Wise and grave men, who, while their diligent
hands
Tendered or gathered in the fruits of earth,
Were reverent learners in the solemn school
Of nature.   Not in vain to them were sent
Seed-time and harvest, or the vernal shower
That darkened the brown tilth, or snow that
beat
On the white winter hills.   Each brought, in
turn,
Some truth, some lesson on the life of man,
Or recognition of the Eternal mind
Who veils his glory with the elements.

One such I knew long since, a white-haired
man,
Pithy of speech, and merry when he would;
A genial optimist, who daily drew
From what he saw his quaint moralities.
Kindly he held communion, though so old,
With me a dreaming boy, and taught me
much
That books tell not, and I shall ne'er forget.

The sun of May was bright in middle heaven,
And steeped the sprouting forests, the green
  hills
And emerald wheat-fields, in his yellow light.
Upon the apple-tree, where rosy buds
Stood clustered, ready to burst forth in bloom,
The robin warbled forth his full clear note
For hours, and wearied not.   Within the
  woods,
Whose young and half transparent leaves scarce
  cast
A shade, gay circles of anemones
Danced on their stalks; the shadbush, white
  with flowers,
Brightened the glens; the new-leaved butter-
  nut
And quivering poplar to the roving breeze
Gave a balsamic fragrance.   In the fields
I saw the pulses of the gentle wind
On the young grass.   My heart was touched
  with joy
At so much beauty, flushing every hour
Into a fuller beauty; but my friend,
The thoughtful ancient, standing at my side,
Gazed on it mildly sad.   I asked him why.

" Well may'st thou join in gladness," he re-
    plied,
" With the glad earth, her springing plants and
    flowers,
And this soft wind, the herald of the green
Luxuriant summer. Thou art young like
    them,
And well may'st thou rejoice. But while the
    flight
Of seasons fills and knits thy spreading frame,
It withers mine, and thins my hair, and dims
These eyes, whose fading light shall soon be
    quenched
In utter darkness. Hearest thou that bird ?"

    I listened, and from 'midst the depth ot
    woods
Heard the love-signal of the grouse, that wears
A sable ruff around his mottled neck ;
Partridge they call him by our northern streams,
And pheasant by the Delaware. He beat
 Gainst his barred sides his speckled wings, and
    made
A sound like distant thunder ; slow the strokes
At first, then faster and faster, till at length
They passed into a murmur and were still.

" There hast thou," said my friend, " a fitting
    type
Of human life.   'Tis an old truth, I know,   ·
But images like these revive the power
Of long familiar truths.   Slow pass our days
In childhood, and the hours of light are long
Betwixt the morn and eve ; with swifter lapse
They glide in manhood, and in age they fly ;
Till days and seasons flit before the mind
As flit the snow-flakes in a winter storm,
Seen rather than distinguished.   Ah ! I seem
As if I sat within a helpless bark,
By swiftly running waters hurried on
To shoot some mighty cliff.   Along the banks
Grove after grove, rock after frowning rock,
Bare sands and pleasant homes, and flowery
    nooks,
And isles and whirlpools in the stream, appear
Each after each, but the devoted skiff
Darts by so swiftly that their images
Dwell not upon the mind, or only dwell
In dim confusion ; faster yet I sweep
By other banks and the great gulf is near.

" Wisely, my son, while yet thy days are
    long,
And this fair change of seasons passes slow,

Gather and treasure up the good they yield—
All that they teach of virtue, of pure thoughts
And kind affections, reverence for thy God
And for thy brethren; so when thou shalt come
Into these barren years, thou may'st not bring
A mind unfurnished and a withered heart.''

Long since that white-haired ancient slept—
    but still,
When the red flower-buds crowd the orchard
    bough,
And the ruffed grouse is drumming far within
The woods, his venerable form again
Is at my side, his voice is in my ear.

AN EVENING REVERIE.

(FROM AN UNFINISHED POEM.)

THE summer day is closed—the sun is set:
Well they have done their office, those bright
    hours,
The latest of whose train goes softly out
In the red West. The green blade of the
    ground
Has risen, and herds have cropped it; the
    young twig

Has spread its plaited tissues to the sun;
Flowers of the garden and the waste have
    blown
And withered; seeds have fallen upon the soil,
From bursting cells, and in their graves await
Their resurrection. Insects from the pools
Have filled the air awhile with humming wings,
That now are still forever; painted moths
Have wandered the blue sky, and died again;
The mother-bird hath broken, for her brood,
Their prison shell, or shoved them from the
    nest,
Plumed for their earliest flight. In bright
    alcoves,
In woodland cottages with barky walls,
In noisome cells of the tumultuous town,
Mothers have clasped with joy the new-born
    babe.
Graves by the lonely forest, by the shore
Of rivers and of ocean, by the ways
Of the thronged city, have been hollowed out
And filled, and closed. This day hath parted
    friends
That ne'er before were parted; it hath knit
New friendships; it hath seen the maiden
    plight
Her faith, and trust her peace to him who long

Had wooed ; and it hath heard, from lips which
    late
Were eloquent of love, the first harsh word,
That told the wedded one her peace was flown.
Farewell to the sweet sunshine! One glad day
Is added now to Childhood's merry days,
And one calm day to those of quiet Age.
Still the fleet hours run on ; and as I lean,
Amid the thickening darkness, lamps are lit,
By those who watch the dead, and those who
    twine
Flowers for the bride. The mother from the
    eyes
Of her sick infant shades the painful light,
And sadly listens to his quick-drawn breath.
   Oh thou great Movement of the Universe,
Or Change, or Flight of Time—for ye are
    one !
That bearest, silently, this visible scene
Into night's shadow and the streaming rays
Of starlight, whither art thou bearing me ?
I feel the mighty current sweep me on,
Yet know not whither. Man foretells afar
The courses of the stars ; the very hour
He knows when they shall darken or grow
    bright ;
Yet doth the eclipse of Sorrow and of Death

Come unforewarned. Who next, of those I
    love,
Shall pass from life, or, sadder yet, shall fall
From virtue? Strife with foes, or bitterer strife
With friends, or shame and general scorn of
    men—
Which who can bear?—or the fierce rank of
    pain,
Lie they within my path? Or shall the years
Push me, with soft and inoffensive pace,
Into the stilly twilight of my age?
Or do the portals of another life
Even now, while I am glorying in my strength,
Impend around me? Oh! beyond that bourne,
In the vast cycle of being which begins
At that dread threshold, with what fairer forms
Shall the great law of change and progress
    clothe
Its workings? Gently—so have good men
    taught—
Gently, and without grief, the old shall glide
Into the new; the eternal flow of things,
Like a bright river of the fields of heaven,
Shall journey onward in perpetual peace.

THE ANTIQUITY OF FREEDOM.

HERE are old trees, tall oaks and gnarled
    pines,
That stream with gray-green mosses ; here the
    ground
Was never trench'd by spade, and flowers
    spring up
Unsown, and die ungathered. It is sweet
To linger here, among the flittering birds,
And leaping squirrels, wandering brooks, and
    winds
That shake the leaves, and scatter as they pass,
A fragrance from the cedars, thickly set
With pale blue berries. In these peaceful
    shades—
Peaceful, unpruned, immeasurably old—
My thoughts go up the long dim path of years,
Back to the earliest days of liberty.

Oh FREEDOM ! thou art not, as poets dream,
A fair young girl, with light and delicate limbs,
And wavy tresses gushing from the cap
With which the Roman master crowned his
    slave
When he took off the gyves. A bearded man,
Armed to the teeth, art thou ; one mailed hand

Grasps the broad shield, and one the sword;
    thy brow,
Glorious in beauty though it be, is scarred
With tokens of old wars; thy massive limbs
Are strong with struggling. Power at thee has
    launched
His bolts, and with his lightnings smitten thee;
They could not quench the life thou hast from
    heaven.
Merciless power has dug thy dungeon deep,
And his swart armorers, by a thousand fires,
Have forged thy chain; yet, while he deems
    thee bound,
The links are shivered, and the prison walls
Fall outward: terribly thou springest forth,
As springs the flame above a burning pile,
And shoutest to the nations, who return
Thy shoutings, while the pale oppressor flies.

   Thy birthright was not given by human
    hands:
Thou wert twin-born with man. In pleasant
    fields,
While yet our race was few, thou sat'st with
    him,
To tend the quiet flock and watch the stars,
And teach the reed to utter simple airs.

Thou by his side, amid the tangled wood,
Didst war upon the panther and the wolf,
His only foes; and thou with him didst draw
The earliest furrows on the mountain side,
Soft with the deluge. Tyranny himself,
Thy enemy, although of reverend look,
Hoary with many years, and far obeyed,
Is later born than thou; and as he meets
The grave defiance of thine elder eye,
The usurper trembles in his fastnesses.

Thou shalt wax stronger with the lapse of
    years,
But he shall fade into a feebler age;
Feebler, yet subtler. He shall weave his snares,
And spring them on thy careless steps, and clap
His withered hands, and from their ambush call
His hordes to fall upon thee. He shall send
Quaint maskers, forms of fair and gallant mien,
To catch thy gaze, and uttering graceful words
To charm thy ear; while his sly imps, by
    stealth,
Twine around thee threads of steel, light thread
    on thread,
That grow to fetters; or bind down thy arms
With chains concealed in chaplets. Oh! not
    yet

May'st thou unbrace thy corselet, nor lay by
Thy sword; nor yet, O Freedom! close thy lids
In slumber; for thine enemy never sleeps,
And thou must watch and combat till the day
Of the new earth and heaven. But wouldst
    thou rest
Awhile from tumult and the frauds of men,
These old and friendly solitudes invite
Thy visit. They, while yet the forest trees
Were young upon the unviolated earth,
And yet the moss-stains on the rock were new,
Beheld thy glorious childhood, and rejoiced.

A HYMN OF THE SEA.

THE sea is mighty, but a mightier sways
His restless billows. Thou whose hands have
    scooped
His boundless gulfs and built his shore, thy
    breath,
That moved in the beginning o'er his face,
Moves o'er it evermore. The obedient waves
To its strong motion roll, and rise and fall.
Still from that realm of rain thy cloud goes up,
As at the first, to water the great earth,
And keep her valleys green. A hundred realms

Watch its broad shadow warping on the wind,
And in the dropping shower, with gladness hear
Thy promise of the harvest.   I look forth
Over the boundless blue, where joyously
The bright crests of innumerable waves
Glance to the sun at once, as when the hands
Of a great multitude are upward flung
In acclamation.   I behold the ships
Gliding from cape to cape, from isle to isle,
Or stemming toward far lands, or hastening
        home
From the Old World.   It is thy friendly breeze
That bears them, with the riches of the land,
And treasure of dear lives, till, in the port,
The shouting seaman climbs and furls the sail.

But who shall bide thy tempest, who shall
        face
The blast that wakes the fury of the sea?
Oh God! thy justice makes the world turn pale,
When on the armed fleet, that royally
Bears down the surges, carrying war, to smite
Some city, or invade some thoughtless realm,
Descends the fierce tornado.   The vast hulks
Are whirled like chaff upon the waves; the sails
Fly, rent like webs of gossamer; the masts

Are snapped asunder; downward from the
    decks,
Downward are slung, into the fathomless gulf,
Their cruel engines; and their hosts, arrayed
In trappings of the battle-field, are whelmed
By whirlpools, or dashed dead upon the rocks.
Then stand tne nations still with awe, and
    pause,
A moment, from the bloody work of war.

These restless surges eat away the shores
Of earth's old continents; the fertile plain
Welters in shallows, headlands crumble down,
And the tide drifts the sea-sand in the streets
Of the drowned city. Thou, meanwhile, afar
In the green chambers of the middle sea,
Where broadest spread the waters and the line
Sinks deepest, while no eye beholds thy work,
Creator! thou dost teach the coral worm
To lay his mighty reefs. From age to age,
He builds beneath the waters, till, at last,
His bulwarks overtop the brine, and check
The long wave rolling from the southern pole
To break upon Japan. Thou bid'st the fires,
That smoulder under ocean, heave on high
The new-made mountains, and uplift their
    peaks,

A place of refuge for the storm-driven bird.
The birds and wafting billows plant the rifts
With herb and tree; sweet fountains gush;
    sweet airs
Ripple the living lakes that, fringed with
    flowers,
Are gathered in the hollows. Thou dost look
On thy creation and pronounce it good.
Its valleys, glorious with their summer green,
Praise thee in silent beauty, and its woods,
Swept by the murmuring winds of ocean, join
The murmuring shores in a perpetual hymn.

THE STREAM OF LIFE.

Oh silvery streamlet of the fields,
    That flowest full and free !
For thee the rains of spring return,
    The summer dews for thee;
And when thy latest blossoms die
    In autumn's chilly showers,
The winter fountains gush for thee,
    Till May brings back the flowers.

Oh Stream of Life! the violet springs
　　But once beside thy bed;
But one brief summer, on thy path,
　　The dews of heaven are shed.
Thy parent fountains shrink away,
　　And close their crystal veins,
And where thy glittering current flowed
　　The dust alone remains.

MIDSUMMER.

(A SONNET.)

A POWER is on the earth and in the air,
　　From which the vital spirit shrinks afraid,
　　And shelters him, in nooks of deepest shade,
From the hot stream and from the fiery glare.
Look forth upon the earth — her thousand
　　　plants
　　Are smitten; even the dark sun-loving
　　　maize
　　Faints in the field beneath the torrid blaze;
The herd beside the shaded fountain pants;
For life is driven from all the landscape brown;
　　The bird has sought his tree, the snake his
　　　den,

The trout floats dead in the hot stream, and
   men
Drop by the sun-stroke in the populace town
   As if the Day of Fire had dawned, and sent
   Its deadly breath into the firmament.

GREEN RIVER.

WHEN breezes are soft and skies are fair,
I steal an hour from study and care,
And hie me away to the woodland scene,
Where wanders the stream with waters of
   green.
As if the bright fringe of herbs on its brink
Had given their stain to the wave they drink;
And they, whose meadows it murmurs through,
Have named the stream from its own fair hue.

Yet pure its waters—its shallows are bright
With coloured pebbles and sparkles of light,
And clear the depths where its eddies play,
And dimples deepen and whirl away,
And the plane-tree's speckled arms o'ershoot
The swifter current that mines its root,
Through whose shifting leaves, as you walk
   the hill,
The quivering glimmer of sun and rill

With a sudden flash on the eye is thrown,
Like the ray that streams from the diamond
    stone.
Oh, loveliest there the spring days come,
With blossoms, and birds, and wild bees' hum;
The flowers of summer are fairest there,
And freshest the breath of the summer air;
And sweetest the golden autumn day
In silence and sunshine glides away.

Yet fair as thou art, thou shunnest to glide,
Beautiful stream! by the village side;
But windest away from haunts of men,
To quiet valley and shaded glen;
And forest, and meadow, and slope of hill,
Around thee, are lonely, lovely, and still.
Lonely—save when, by thy rippling tides,
From thicket to thicket the angler glides;
Or the simpler comes with basket and book,
For herbs of power on thy banks to look;
Or haply, some idle dreamer, like me,
To wander, and muse, and gaze on thee.
Still—save the chirp of birds that feed
On the river cherry and seedy reed,
And thy own wild music gushing out
With mellow murmur and fairy shout,

From dawn to the blush of another day,
Like traveller singing along his way.

That fairy music I never hear,
Nor gaze on those waters so green and clear,
And mark them winding away from sight.
Darkened with shade or flashing with light,
While o'er them the vine to its thicket clings,
And the zephyr stoops to freshen his wings,
But I wish that fate had left me free
To wander these quiet haunts with thee,
Till the eating cares of earth should depart,
And the peace of the scene pass into my heart ;
And I envy thy stream, as it glides along,
Through its beautiful banks in a trance of song.

Though forced to drudge for the dregs of men,
And scrawl strange words with the barbarous
    pen,
And mingle among the jostling crowd,
Where the sons of strife are subtle and loud—
I often come to this quiet place,
To breathe the airs that ruffle thy face,
And gaze upon thee in silent dream,
For in thy lonely and lovely stream
An image of that calm life appears
That won my heart in my greener years.

10

A WINTER PIECE.

THE time has been that these wild solitudes,
Yet beautiful as wild, were trod by me
Oftener than now ; and when the ills of life
Had chafed my spirit—when the unsteady
　　pulse
Beat with strange flutterings—I would wander
　　forth
And seek the woods. The sunshine on my
　　path
Was to me as a friend. The swelling hills,
The quiet dells retiring far between,
With gentle invitation to explore
Their windings, were a calm society
That talked with me and soothed me. Then
　　the chant
Of birds, and chime of brooks, and soft caress
Of the fresh sylvan air, made me forget
The thoughts that broke my peace, and I began
To gather simples by the fountain's brink,
And lose myself in day-dreams. While I stood
In nature's loneliness, I was with one
With whom I early grew familiar, one
Who never had a frown for me, whose voice
Never rebuked me for the hours I stole
From cares I loved not, but of which the world

Deems highest, to converse with her. When
    shrieked
The bleak November winds, and smote the
    woods,
And the brown fields were herbless, and the
    shades,
That met above the merry rivulet,
Were spoiled, I sought, I loved them still,—
    they seemed
Like old companions in adversity.
Still there was beauty in my walks; the brook,
Bordered with sparkling frost-work, was as
    gay
As with its fringe of summer flowers. Afar,
The village with its spires, the path of streams,
And dim receding valleys, hid before
By interposing trees, lay visible
Through the bare grove, and my familiar
    haunts
Seemed new to me. Nor was I slow to come
Among them, when the clouds, from their still
    skirts,
Had shaken down on earth the feathery snow,
And all was white. The pure keen air abroad,
Albeit it breathed no scent of herb, nor heard
Love-call of bird nor merry hum of bee,
Was not the air of death. Bright mosses crept

Over the spotted trunks, and the close buds,
That lay along the boughs, instinct with life,
Patient and waiting the soft breath of Spring,
Feared not the piercing spirit of the North. .
The snow-bird twittered on the beechen bough,
And 'neath the hemlock, whose thick branches
　　bent
Beneath its bright cold burden, and kept dry
A circle, on the earth, of withered leaves,
The partridge found a shelter. Through the
　　snow
The rabbit sprang away. The lighter track
Of fox, and the racoon's broad path, were there,
Crossing each other. From his hollow tree,
The squirrel was abroad, gathering the nuts
Just fallen, that asked the winter cold and sway
Of winter blast, to shake them from their hold.

　　But Winter has yet brighter scenes, — he
　　　boasts
Splendours beyond what gorgeous Summer
　　　knows ;
Or Autumn with his many fruits, and woods
All flushed with many hues. Come when the
　　　rains
Have glazed the snow, and clothed the trees
　　　with ice ;

While the slant sun of February pours
Into the bowers a flood of light.   Approach!
The incrusted surface shall upbear thy steps,
And the broad arching portals of the grove
Welcome thy entering.   Look! the massy
 trunks
Are cased in the pure crystal; each light spray,
Nodding and tinkling in the breath of heaven,
Is studded with its trembling water-drops,
That stream with rainbow radiance as they
 move.
But round the parent stem the long low boughs
Bend, in a glittering ring, and arbours hide
The glassy floor.   Oh! you might deem the
 spot
The spacious cavern of some virgin mine,
Deep in the womb of earth—where the gems
 grow,
And diamonds put forth radiant rods and bud
With amethyst and topaz—and the place
Lit up, most royally, with the pure beam
That dwells in them.   Or haply the vast hall
Of fairy palace, that outlasts the night,
And fades not in the glory of the sun ;—
Where crystal columns send forth slender
 shafts
And crossing arches ; and fantastic aisles

Wind from the sight in brightness, and are lost
Among the crowded pillars. Raise thine eye,—
Thou seest no cavern roof, no palace vault;
There the blue sky and the white drifting cloud
Look in. Again the wildered fancy dreams
Of spouting fountains, frozen as they rose,
And fixed, with all their branching jets, in air,
And all their sluices sealed. All, all is light;
Light without shade. But all shall pass away
With the next sun. From numberless vast
    trunks,
Loosened, the crashing ice shall make a sound
Like the far roar of rivers, and the eve
Shall close o'er the brown woods as it was wont.

And it is pleasant, when the noisy streams
Are just set free, and milder suns melt off
The plashy snow, save only the firm drift
In the deep glen or the close shade of pines,—
'Tis pleasant to behold the wreaths of smoke
Roll up among the maples of the hill,
Where the shrill sound of youthful voices wakes
The shriller echo, as the clear pure lymph,
That from the wounded trees, in twinkling
    drops,
Falls, mid the golden brightness of the morn,
Is gathered in with brimming pails, and oft,

Wielded by sturdy hands, the stroke of axe
Makes the woods ring.   Along the quiet air,
Come and float calmly off the soft light clouds,
Such as you see in summer, and the winds
Scarce stir the branches.   Lodged in sunny
    cleft,
Where the cold breezes come not, blooms alone
The little-wind flower, whose just opened eye
Is blue as the spring heaven it gazes at—
Startling the loiterer in the naked groves
With unexpected beauty, for the time
Of blossoms and green leaves is yet afar.
And ere it comes, the encountering winds shall
    oft
Muster their wrath again, and rapid clouds
Shade heaven, and bounding on the frozen
    earth
Shall fall their volleyed stores rounded like
    hail,
And white like snow, and the loud North again
Shall buffet the vexed forest in his rage.

HYMN TO DEATH.

OH! could I hope the wise and pure in heart
Might hear my song without a frown, nor deem
My voice unworthy of the theme it tries,—

I would take up the hymn to Death, and say
To the grim power, The world hath slandered
    thee
And mocked thee. On thy dim and shadowy
    brow
They place an iron crown, and call thee king
Of terrors, and the spoiler of the world,
Deadly assassin, that strik'st down the fair,
The loved, the good—that breathest on the
    lights
Of virtue set along the vale of life,
And they go out in darkness. I am come,
Not with reproaches, not with cries and prayers,
Such as have stormed thy stern, insensible ear
From the beginning. I am come to speak
Thy praises. True it is, that I have wept
Thy conquests, and may weep them yet again:
And thou from some I love wilt take a life
Dear to me as my own. Yet while the spell
Is on my spirit, and I talk with thee
In sight of all thy trophies, face to face,
Meet is it that my voice should utter forth
Thy nobler triumphs; I will teach the world
To thank thee.—Who are thine accusers?—
    Who?
The living!—they who never felt thy power,
And know thee not. The curses of the wretch

Whose crimes are ripe, his sufferings when thy
    hand
Is on him, and the hour he dreads is come,
Are writ among thy praises. But the good—
Does he whom thy kind hand dismissed to
    peace,
Upbraid the gentle violence that took off
His fetters, and unbarred his prison cell?

    Raise then the hymn to death. Deliverer!
God hath anointed thee to free the oppressed
And crush the oppressor. When the armed
    chief,
The conqueror of nations, walks the world,
And it is changed beneath his feet, and all
Its kingdoms melt into one mighty realm—
Thou, while his head is loftiest and his heart
Blasphemes, imagining his own right hand
Almighty, thou dost set thy sudden grasp
Upon him, and the links of that strong chain
That bound mankind are crumbled; thou dost
    break
Sceptre and crown, and beat his throne to dust.
Then the earth shouts with gladness, and her
    tribes
Gather within their ancient bounds again.
Else had the mighty of the olden time,

Nimrod, Sesostris, or the youth who feigned
His birth from Libyan Ammon, smitten yet
The nations with a rod of iron, and driven
Their chariot o'er our necks. Thou dost
    avenge,
In thy good time, the wrongs of those who
    know
No other friend. Nor dost thou interpose
Only to lay the sufferer asleep,
Where he who made him wretched troubles
    not
His rest—thou dost strike down his tyrant too.
Oh, there is joy when hands that held the
    scourge
Drop lifeless, and the pitiless heart is cold
Thou too dost purge from earth its horrible
And old idolatries ;—from the proud fanes
Each to his grave their priests go out, till none
Is left to teach their worship ; then the fires
Of sacrifice are chilled, and the green moss
O'ercreeps their altars ; the fallen images
Cumber the weedy courts, and for loud hymns,
Chanted by kneeling multitudes, the wind
Shrieks in the solitary aisles. When he
Who gives his life to guilt, and laughs at all
The laws that God or man has made, and
    round

Hedges his seat with power, and shines in
    wealth,—
Lifts up his atheist front to scoff at Heaven,
And celebrates his shame in open day,
Thou, in the pride of all his crimes, cutt'st off
The horrible example. Touched by thine,
The extortioner's hard hand foregoes the gold
Wrung from the o'er-worn poor. The perjurer,
Whose tongue was lithe, e'en now, and voluble
Against his neighbour's life, and he who
    laughed
And leaped for joy to see a spotless fame
Blasted before his own foul calumnies,
Are smit with deadly silence. He, who sold
His conscience to preserve a worthless life,
Even while he hugs himself on his escape,
Trembles, as, doubly terrible, at length,
Thy steps o'ertake him, and there is no time
For parley—nor will bribes unclench thy grasp.
Oft, too, dost thou reform thy victim, long
Ere his last hour. And when the reveller,
Mad in the chase of pleasure, stretches on,
And strains each nerve, and clears the path of
    life
Like wind, thou point'st him to the dreadful
    goal,
And shak'st thy hour-glass in his reeling-eye,

And check'st him in mid course. Thy skeleton
    hand
Shows to the faint of spirit the right path,
And he is warned, and fears to step aside.
Thou sett'st between the ruffian and his crime
Thy ghastly countenance, and his slack hand
Drops the drawn knife. But, oh, most fearfully
Dost thou show forth Heaven's justice, when
    thy shafts
Drink up the ebbing spirit—then the hard
Of heart and violent of hand restores
The treasure to the friendless wretch he
    wronged.
Then from the writhing bosom thou dost pluck
The guilty secret; lips, for ages sealed,
Are faithless to the dreadful trust at length,
And give it up; the felon's latest breath
Absolves the innocent man who bears his
    crime;
The slanderer, horror-smitten, and in tears,
Recalls the deadly obloquy he forged
To work his brother's ruin. Thou dost make
Thy penitent victim utter to the air
The dark conspiracy that strikes at life,
And aims to whelm the laws; ere yet the hour
Is come, and the dread sign of murder given.

Thus, from the first of time, hast thou been
    found
On virtue's side! the wicked, but for thee,
Had been too strong for the good; the great of
    earth
Had crushed the weak for ever.   Schooled in
    guile
For ages, while each passing year had brought
Its baneful lesson, they had filled the world
With their abominations; while its tribes,
Trodden to earth, imbruted, and despoiled,
Had knelt to them in worship; sacrifice
Had smoked on many an altar, temple roofs
Had echoed with the blasphemous prayer and
    hymn:
But thou, the great reformer of the world,
Tak'st off the sons of violence and fraud
In their green pupilage, their lore half learned—
Ere guilt had quite o'errun the simple heart
God gave them at their birth, and blotted out
His image.   Thou dost mark them flushed with
    hope,
As on the threshold of their vast designs
Doubtful and loose they stand, and strik'st them
    down.

    *

Alas ! I little thought that the stern power
Whose fearful praise I sung, would try me thus
Before the strain was ended.   It must cease—
For he is in his grave who taught my youth
The art of verse, and in the bud of life
Offered me to the muses.   Oh, cut off
Untimely ! when thy reason in its strength,
Ripened by years of toil and studious search,
And watch of Nature's silent lessons, taught
Thy hand to practice best the lenient art,
To which thou gavest thy laborious days,
And, last, thy life.   And, therefore, when the
      earth
Received thee, tears were in unyielding eyes
And on hard cheeks, and they who deemed thy
      skill
Delayed their death-hour, shuddered and turned
      pale
When thou wert gone.   This faltering verse,
      which thou
Shalt not, as wont, o'erlook, is all I have
To offer at thy grave—this—and the hope
To copy thy example, and to leave
A name of which the wretched shall not think
As of an enemy's, whom they forgive
As all forgive the dead.   Rest, therefore, thou
Whose early guidance trained my infant steps—

Rest, in the bosom of God, till the brief sleep
Of death is over, and a happier life
Shall dawn to waken thine insensible dust.

Now thou art not—and yet the men whose
guilt
Has wearied Heaven for vengeance—he who
bears
False witness—he who takes the orphan's bread,
And robs the widow—he who spreads abroad
Polluted hands of mockery of prayer,
Are left to cumber earth.   Shuddering I look
On what is written, yet I blot not out
The desultory numbers—let them stand,
The record of an idle revery.

LINES ON REVISITING THE COUNTRY.

I STAND upon my native hills again,
  Broad, round, and green, that in the sum-
  mer sky
With garniture of waving grass and grain,
  Orchards, and beechen forests, basking lie,
While deep the sunless glens are scooped be-
  tween,
Where brawl o'er shallow beds the streams un-
  seen.

A lisping voice and glancing eyes are near,
   And ever restless feet of one, who, now,
Gathers the blossoms of her fourth bright year;
   There plays a gladness o'er her fair young
     brow,
As breaks the varied scene upon her sight,
Upheaved and spread in verdure and in light.

For I have taught her, with delighted eye,
   To gaze upon the mountains,—to behold,
With deep affection, the pure ample sky,
   And clouds along its blue abysses rolled,—
To love the song of waters, and to hear
The melody of winds with charmed ear.

Here, I have 'scaped the city's stifling heat,
   Its horrid sounds, and its polluted air;
And, where the season's milder fervours beat,
   And gales, that sweep the forest borders,
     bear
The song of bird, and sound of running stream,
Am come awhile to wander and to dream.

Ay, flame thy fiercest, sun! thou canst **not**
     wake,
   In this pure air the plague that walks un-
     seen.

The maize leaf and the maple bough but take,
  From thy strong heats, a deeper, glossier
    green.
The mountain wind, that faints not in thy ray
Sweeps the blue streams of pestilence away.

The mountain wind! most spiritual thing of all
  The wide earth knows; when, in the sultry
    time,
He stoops him from his vast cerulean hall,
  He seems the breath of a celestial clime!
As if from heaven's wide-open gates did flow
Health and refreshment on the world below.

"UPON THE MOUNTAIN'S DISTANT HEAD."

Upon the mountain's distant head,
  With trackless snows for ever white,
Where all is still, and cold, and dead,
  Late shines the day's departing light.

But far below those icy rocks,
  The vales, in summer bloom arrayed,
Woods full of birds, and fields of flocks,
  Are dim with mist and dark with shade.

'Tis thus, from warm and kindly hearts,
　And eyes where generous meanings burn,
Earliest the light of life departs,
　But lingers with the cold and stern.

THE JOURNEY OF LIFE.

BENEATH the waning moon I walk at night,
　And muse on human life—for all around
Are dim uncertain shapes that cheat the sight,
　And pitfalls lurk in shade along the ground,
And broken gleams of brightness, here and
　　there,
Glance through, and leave unwarmed the
　　death-like air.

The trampled earth returns a sound of fear—
　A hollow sound, as if I walked on tombs;
And lights, that tell of cheerful homes, appear
　Far off, and die like hope amid the glooms.
A mournful wind across the landscape flies,
And the wide atmosphere is full of sighs.

And I, with faltering footsteps, journey on,
　Watching the stars that roll the hours away,

Till the faint light that guides me now is gone,
 And, like another life, the glorious day
Shall open o'er me from the empyreal height,
With warmth, and certainty, and boundless
 light.

LOVE AND FOLLY.

(FROM LA FONTAINE.)

LOVE'S worshippers alone can know
 The thousand mysteries that are his;
His blazing torch, his twanging bow,
 His blooming age are mysteries.
A charming science—but the day
 Were all too short to con it o'er;
So take of me this little lay,
 A sample of its boundless lore.

As once, beneath the fragrant shade
 Of myrtles breathing heaven's own air,
The children, Love and Folly, played—
 A quarrel rose betwixt the pair.
Love said the gods should do him right—
 But Folly vowed to do it then,
And struck him, o'er the orbs of sight,
 So hard he never saw again.

His lovely mother's grief was deep,
  She called for vengeance on the deed;
A beauty does not vainly weep,
  Nor coldly does a mother plead.
A shade came o'er the eternal bliss
  That fills the dwellers of the skies;
Even stony-hearted Nemesis,
  And Rhadamanthus, wiped their eyes.

"Behold," she said, "this lovely boy,"
  While streamed afresh her graceful tears,
"Immortal, yet shut out from joy
  And sunshine, all his future years.
The child can never take, you see,
  A single step without a staff—
The harshest punishment would be
  Too lenient for the crime by half."

All said that Love had suffered wrong,
  And well that wrong should be repaid;
Then weighed the public interest long,
  And long the party's interest weighed.
And thus decreed the court above—
  "Since Love is blind from Folly's blow,
Let Folly be the guide of Love,
  Where'er the boy may choose to go."

THE LOVE OF GOD.

(FROM THE PROVENCAL OF BERNARD RASCAS.)

ALL things that are on earth shall wholly
    pass away,
Except the love of God, which shall live and
    last for aye.
The forms of men shall be as they had never
    been ;
The blasted groves shall lose their fresh and
    tender green ;
The birds of the thicket shall end their pleasant
    song,
And the nightingale shall cease to chant the
    evening long.
The kine of the pasture shall feel the dart that
    kills,
And all the fair white flocks shall perish from
    the hills.
The goat and antlered stag, the wolf and the
    fox,
The wild boar of the wood, and the chamois of
    the rocks,
And the strong and fearless bear, in the trodden
    dust shall lie ;
And the dolphin of the sea, and the mighty
    whale, shall die.

And realms shall be dissolved, and empires be
    no more,
And they shall bow to death, who ruled from
    shore to shore;
And the great globe itself, (so the holy writings
    tell,)
With the rolling firmament, where the starry
    armies dwell,
Shall melt with fervent heat—they shall all
    pass away,
Except the love of God, which shall live and
    last for aye.

EARTH.

A MIDNIGHT black with clouds is in the sky;
I seem to feel, upon my limbs, the weight
Of its vast brooding shadow.   All in vain
Turns the tired eye in search of form; no star
Pierces the pitchy veil; no ruddy blaze,
From dwellings lighted by the cheerful hearth,
Tinges the flowering summits of the grass.
No sound of life is heard, no village hum,
Nor measured tramp of footstep in the path,
Nor rush of wing, while, on the breast of Earth,
I lie and listen to her mighty voice:

A voice of many tones—sent up from streams
That wander through the gloom, from woods
 unseen,
Swayed by the sweeping of the tides of air,
From rocky chasms where darkness dwells all
 day,
And hollows of the great invisible hills,
And sands that edge the ocean, stretching far
Into the night—a melancholy sound!

O Earth! dost thou too sorrow for the past
Like man thy offspring? Do I hear thee mourn
Thy childhood's unreturning hours, thy springs
Gone with their genial airs and melodies,
The gentle generations of thy flowers,
And thy majestic groves of olden time,
Perished with all their dwellers? Dost thou
 wail
For that fair age of which the poets tell,
Ere the rude winds grew keen with frost, or fire
Fell with the rains, or spouted from the hills,
To blast thy greenness, while the virgin night
Was guiltless and salubrious as the day?
Or haply dost thou grieve for those that die—
For living things that trod thy paths awhile,
The love of thee and heaven—and now they
 sleep

Mixed with the shapeless dust on which thy
    herds
Trample and graze? I too must grieve with
    thee,
O'er loved ones lost. Their graves are far
    away
Upon thy mountains; yet, while I recline
Alone, in darkness, on thy naked soil,
The mighty nourisher and burial-place
Of man, I feel that I embrace their dust.

Ha! how the murmur deepens! I perceive
And tremble at its dreadful import.   Earth
Uplifts a general cry for guilt and wrong,
And heaven is listening.   The forgotten grave
Of the heart-broken utter forth their plaint.
The dust of her who loved and was betrayed,
And him who died neglected in his age;
The sepulchres of those who for mankind
Laboured, and earned the recompense of scorn .
Ashes of martyrs for the truth, and bones
Of those who, in the strife for liberty,
Were beaten down, their corses given to dogs,
Their names to infamy, all find a voice.
The nook in which the captive, overtoiled,
Lay down to rest at last, and that which holds

Childhood's sweet blossoms, crushed by cruel
    hands,
Send up a plaintive sound. From battle-fields,
Where heroes madly drave and dashed their
    hosts
Against each other, rises up a noise,
As if the armed multitudes of dead
Stirred in their heavy slumber. Mournful tones
Come from the green abysses of the sea—
A story of the crimes the guilty sought
To hide beneath its waves. The glens, the
    groves,
Paths in the thicket, pools of running brook,
And banks and depths of lake, and streets and
    lanes
Of cities, now that living sounds are hushed,
Murmur of guilty force and treachery.

    Here, where I rest, the vales of Italy
Are round me, populous from early time,
And field of the tremendous warfare waged
'Twixt good and evil. Who, alas, shall dare
Interpret to man's ear the mingled voice
That comes from her old dungeons yawning now
To the black air, her amphitheatres,
Where the dew gathers on the mouldering
    stones,

And fanes of banished gods, and open tombs,
And roofless palaces, and streets and hearths
Of cities dug from their volcanic graves?
I hear a sound of many languages,
The utterance of nations now no more,
Driven out by mightier, as the days of heaven
Chase one another from the sky.   The blood
Of freemen shed by freemen, till strange lords
Came in the hour of weakness, and made fast
The yoke that yet is worn, cries out to Heaven.

    What then shall cleanse thy bosom, gentle
       Earth,
From all its painful memories of guilt?
The whelming flood, or the renewing fire,
Or the slow change of time? that so, at last,
The horrid tale of perjury and strife,
Murder and spoil, which men call history,
May seem a fable, like the inventions told
By poets of the gods of Greece.   O thou,
Who sittest far beyond the Atlantic deep,
Among the sources of thy glorious streams,
My native Land of Groves! a newer page
In the great record of the world is thine;
Shall it be fairer? Fear, and friendly hope,
And envy, watch the issue, while the lines,
By which thou shalt be judged, are written
      down.

CATTERSKILL FALLS.

Midst greens and shades the Catterskill leaps,
From cliffs where the wood-flower clings;
All summer he moistens his verdant steeps
With the sweet light spray of the mountain
springs;
And he shakes the woods on the mountain side,
When they drip with the rains of autumn-tide.

But when, in the forest bare and old,
The blast of December calls,
He builds, in the starlight clear and cold,
A palace of ice where his torrent falls,
With turret, and arch, and fretwork fair,
And pillars blue as the summer air.

For whom are those glorious chambers wrought,
In the cold and cloudless night?
Is there neither spirit nor motion of thought
In forms so lovely, and hues so bright?
Hear what the gray-haired woodmen tell
Of this wild stream and its rocky dell.

'Twas hither a youth of dreamy mood,
A hundred winters ago,
Had wandered over the mighty wood,

When the panther's track was fresh on the
   snow,
And keen were the winds that came to stir
The long dark boughs of the hemlock fir.

Too gentle of mien he seemed and fair,
   For a child of those rugged steeps ;
His home lay low in the valley where
   The kingly Hudson rolls to the deeps ; .
But he wore the hunter's frock that day,
And a slender gun on his shoulder lay.

And here he paused, and against the trunk
   Of a tall gray linden leant,
When the broad clear orb of the sun had sunk
   From his path in the frosty firmament,
And over the round dark edge of the hill
A cold green light was quivering still.

And the crescent moon, high over the green,
   From a sky of crimson shone,
On that icy palace, whose towers were seen
   To sparkle as if with stars of their own ;
While the water fell with a hollow sound,
'Twixt the glistening pillars ranged around.

Is that a being of life, that moves
   Where the crystal battlements rise ?

A maiden watching the moon she loves,
　At the twilight hour, with pensive eyes ?
Was that a garment which seemed to gleam
Betwixt the eye and the falling stream ?

'Tis only the torrent tumbling o'er,
　In the midst of those glassy walls,
Gushing, and plunging, and beating the fl,or
　Of the rocky basin in which it falls.
'Tis only the torrent—but why that start ?
Why gazes the youth with a throbbing heart ?

He thinks no more of his home afar,
　Where his sire and sister wait.
He heeds no longer how star after star
　Looks forth on the night as the hour grows
　　late.
He heeds not the snow-wreaths, lifted and cast
From a thousand boughs, by the rising blast.

His thoughts are alone of those who dwell
　In the halls of frost and snow,
Who pass where the crystal domes upswell
　From the alabaster floors below,
Where the frost-trees shoot with leaf and spray,
And frost-gems scatter a silvery day.

"And oh that those glorious haunts were mine!"
　He speaks, and throughout the glen
Thin shadows swim in the faint moonshine,
　And take a ghastly likeness of men,
As if the slain by the wintry storms
Came forth to the air in their earthly forms.

There pass the chasers of seal and whale,
　With their weapons quaint and grim,
And bands of warriors in glittering mail,
　And herdsmen and hunters huge of limb.
There are naked arms, with bow and spear,
And furry gauntlets the carbine rear.

There are mothers—and oh how sadly their
　　eyes
　On their children's white brows rest!
There are youthful lovers—the maiden lies,
　In a seeming sleep, on the chosen breast;
There are fair wan women with moonstruck air,
The snow stars flecking their long loose hair.

They eye him not as they pass along,
　But his hair stands up with dread,
When he feels that he moves with that phan-
　　tom throng,
　Till those icy turrets are over his head.

And the torrent's roar as they enter seems
Like a drowsy murmur heard in dreams.

The glittering threshold is scarcely passed,
    When there gathers and wraps him round
A thick white twilight, sullen and vast,
    In which there is neither form nor sound;
The phantoms, the glory, vanish all,
With the dying voice of the waterfall.

Slow passes the darkness of that trance,
    And the youth now faintly sees
Huge shadows and gushes of light that dance
    On a rugged ceiling of unhewn trees,
And walls where the skins of beasts are hung,
And rifles glitter on antlers strung.

On a couch of shaggy skins he lies;
    As he strives to raise his head,
Hard-featured woodmen, with kindly eyes,
    Come round him and smooth his furry bed,
And bid him rest, for the evening star
Is scarcely set and the day is far.

They had found at eve the dreaming one
    By the base of that icy steep,
When over his stiffening limbs begun

The deadly slumber of frost to creep,
And they cherished the pale and breathless
    form,
Till the stagnant blood ran free and warm.

LIFE.

OH Life ! I breathe thee in the breeze,
    I feel thee bounding in my veins,
I see thee in these stretching trees,
    These flowers, this still rock's mossy stains.

This stream of odours flowing by
    From clover-field and clumps of pine,
This music, thrilling all the sky,
    From all the morning birds, are thine.

Thou fill'st with joy this little one,
    That leaps and shouts beside me here,
Where Isar's clay-white rivulets run
    Through the dark woods like frighted deer.

Ah ! must thy mighty breath, that wakes
    Insect and bird, and flower and tree,
From the low trodden dust, and makes
    Their daily gladness, pass from me—

Pass, pulse by pulse, till o'er the ground
    These limbs, now strong, shall creep with
      pain,
And this fair world of sight and sound
    Seem fading into night again?

The things, oh LIFE! thou quickenest, all
    Strive upward toward the broad bright sky,
Upward and outward, and they fall
    Back to earth's bosom when they die.

All that have borne the touch of death,
    All that shall live, lie mingled there,
Beneath that veil of bloom and breath,
    That living zone 'twixt earth and air.

There lies my chamber dark and still,
    The atoms trampled by my feet,
There wait, to take the place I fill
    In the sweet air and sunshine sweet.

Well, I have had my turn, have been
    Raised from the darkness of the clod,
And for a glorious moment seen
    The brightness of the skirts of God;

And knew the light within my breast,
    Though wavering oftentimes and dim,
12

The power, the will, that never rest,
  And cannot die, were all from him.

Dear child! I know that thou wilt grieve
  To see me taken from thy love,
Wilt seek my grave at Sabbath eve,
  And weep, and scatter flowers above.

Thy little heart will soon be healed,
  And being shall be bliss, till thou
To younger forms of life must yield
  The place thou fill'st with beauty now.

When we descend to dust again,
  Where will the final dwelling be
Of Thought and all its memories then,
  My love for thee, and thine for me?

THE FOUNTAIN.

FOUNTAIN, that springest on this grassy slope,
Thy quick cool murmur mingles pleasantly,
With the cool sound of breezes in the beach,
Above me in the noontide. Thou dost wear
No stain of thy dark birthplace; gushing up
From the red mould and slimy roots of earth,
Thou flashest in the sun. The mountain air,

In winter, is not clearer, nor the dew
That shines on mountain blossom. Thus doth
    God
Bring, from the dark and foul, the pure and
    bright.

This tangled thicket on the bank above
Thy basin, how thy waters keep it green!
For thou dost feed the roots of the wild vine
That trails all over it, and to the twigs
Ties fast her clusters. There the spice-bush
    lifts
Her leafy lances; the viburnum there,
Paler of foliage, to the sun holds up
Her circlet of green berries. In and out
The chipping sparrow, in her coat of brown,
Steals silently, lest I should mark her nest.

Not such thou wert of yore, ere yet the axe
Had smitten the old woods. Then hoary
    trunks
Of oak, and plane, and hickory, o'er thee held
A mighty canopy. When April winds
Grew soft, the maple burst into a flush
Of scarlet flowers. The tulip-tree, high up,
Opened, in airs of June, her multitude
Of golden chalices to humming-birds
And silken-winged insects of the sky.

Frail wood-plants clustered round thy edge
   in Spring.
The liverleaf put forth her sister blooms
Of faintest blue.   Here the quick-footed wolf,
Passing to lap thy waters, crushed the flower
Of sanguinaria, from whose brittle stem
The red drops fell like blood.   The deer, too,
   left
Her delicate foot-print in the soft moist mould,
And on the fallen leaves.   The slow-paced
   bear,
In such a sultry summer noon as this,
Stopped at thy stream, and drank, and leaped
   across.

But thou hast histories that stir the heart
With deeper feeling; while I look on thee
They rise before me.   I behold the scene
Hoary again with forests; I behold
The Indian warrior, whom a hand unseen
Has smitten with his death-wound in the woods,
Creep slowly to thy well-known rivulet,
And slake his death-thirst.   Hark, that quick
   fierce cry
That rends the utter silence; 'tis the whoop
Of battle, and a throng of savage men
With naked arms and faces stained like blood,

Fill the green wilderness; the long bare arms
Are heaved aloft, bows twang and arrows
    stream;
Each makes a tree his shield, and every tree
Sends forth its arrow. Fierce the fight and
    short,
As is the whirlwind. Soon the conquerors
And conquered vanish, and the dead remain
Mangled by tomahawks. The mighty woods
Are still again, the frighted bird comes back
And plumes her wings; but thy sweet waters
    run
Crimson with blood. Then, as the sun goes
    down,
Amid the deepening twilight I descry
Figures of men that crouch and creep unheard,
And bear away the dead. The next day's
    shower
Shall wash the tokens of the fight away.

I look again—a hunter's lodge is built,
With poles and boughs, beside thy crystal well,
While the meek autumn stains the woods with
    gold,
And sheds his golden sunshine. To the door
The red man slowly drags the enormous bear
Slain in the chestnut thicket, or flings down

The deer from his strong shoulders. Shaggy
    fells
Of wolf and cougar hang upon the walls,
And loud the black-eyed Indian maidens laugh,
That gather, from the rustling heaps of leaves,
The hickory's white nuts, and the dark fruit
That falls from the gray butternut's long boughs.

  So centuries passed by, and still the woods
Blossomed in spring, and reddened when the
    year
Grew chill, and glistened in the frozen rains
Of winter, till the white man swung the axe
Beside thee—signal of a mighty change.
Then all around was heard the crash of trees,
Trembling awhile and rushing to the ground,
The low of ox, and shouts of men who fired
The brushwood, or who tore the earth with
    ploughs.
The grain sprang thick and tall, and hid in green
The blackened hill-side; ranks of spiky maize
Rose like a host embattled; the buckwheat
Whitened broad acres, sweetening with its
    flowers
The August wind. White cottages were seen
With rose-trees at the windows; barns from
    which

Came loud and shrill the crowing of the cock ;
Pastures where rolled and neighed the lordly
    horse,
And white flocks browsed and bleated. A rich
    turf
Of grasses brought from far o'ercrept thy bank,
Spotted with the white clover. Blue-eyed girls
Brought pails and dipped them in thy crystal
    pool ;
And children, ruddy-cheeked and flaxen-haired,
Gathered the glistening cowslip from thy edge.

    Since then, what steps have trod thy border !
    Here
On thy green bank, the woodman of the swamp
Has laid his axe, the reaper of the hill
His sickle, as they stooped to taste thy stream.
The sportsman, tired with wandering in the still
September noon, has bathed his heated brow
In thy cool current. Shouting boys, let loose
For a wild holiday, have quaintly shaped
Into a cup the folded linden leaf,
And dipped thy sliding crystal. From the wars
Returning, the plumed soldier by thy side
Has sat, and mused how pleasant 'twere to
    dwell
In such a spot, and be as free as thou,

And move for no man's bidding more. At eve,
When thou wert crimson with the crimson sky,
Lovers have gazed upon thee, and have thought
Their mingled lives should flow as peacefully
And brightly as thy waters.   Here the sage,
Gazing into thy self-replenished depth,
Has seen eternal order circumscribe
And bind the motions of eternal change,
And from the gushing of thy simple fount
Has reasoned to the mighty universe.

Is there no other change for thee, that lurks
Among the future ages ?   Will not man
Seek out strange arts to wither and deform
The pleasant landscape which thou makest
    green ?
Or shall the veins that feed thy constant stream
Be choked in middle earth, and flow no more
For ever, that the water-plants along
Thy channel perish, and the bird in vain
Alight to drink ? Haply shall these green hills
Sink, with the lapse of years, into the gulf
Of ocean waters, and thy source be lost
Amidst the bitter brine ?   Or shall they rise,
Upheaved in broken cliffs and airy peaks,
Haunts of the eagle and the snake, and thou
Gush midway from the bare and barren steep ?

SONG.

Soon as the glazed and gleaming snow
　Reflects the day-dawn cold and clear,
The hunter of the west must go
　In depth of woods to seek the deer.

His rifle on his shoulder placed,
　His stores of death arranged with skill,
His moccasins and snow-shoes laced,—
　Why lingers he beside the hill?

Far, in the dim and doubtful light,
　Where woody slopes a valley leave,
He sees what none but lover might,
　The dwelling of his Genevieve.

And oft he turns his truant eye,
　And pauses oft, and lingers near;
But when he marks the reddening sky,
　He bounds away to hunt the deer.

THE WEST WIND.

Beneath the forest's skirts I rest,
　Whose branching pines rise dark and high,
And hear the breezes of the West
　Among the threaded foliage sigh.

Sweet Zephyr! why that sound of woe?
  Is not thy home among the flowers?
Do not the bright June roses blow,
  To meet thy kiss at morning hours?

And lo! thy glorious realm outspread—
  Yon stretching valleys, green and gay,
And yon free hill-tops, o'er whose head
  The loose white clouds are borne away.

And there the full broad river runs,
  And many a fount wells fresh and sweet,
To cool thee when the mid-day suns
  Have made thee faint beneath their heat.

Thou wind of joy, and youth, and love;
  Spirit of the new-wakened year!
The sun in his blue realm above
  Smooths a bright path when thou art here.

In lawns the murmuring bee is heard,
  The wooing ring-dove in the shade;
On thy soft breath, the new-fledged bird
  Takes wing, half happy, half afraid.

Ah! thou art like our wayward race;—
  When not a shade of pain or ill
Dims the bright smile of Nature's face,
  Thou lovest to sigh and murmur still.

THE BURIAL-PLACE.

A FRAGMENT.

Erewhile, on England's pleasant shores, our
    sires
Left not their churchyards unadorned with
    shades
Or blossoms; and indulgent to the strong
And natural dread of man's last home, the grave,
Its frost and silence—they disposed around,
To soothe the melancholy spirit that dwelt
Too sadly on life's close, the forms and hues
Of vegetable beauty.—There the yew
Green even amid the snows of winter, told
Of immortality, and gracefully
The willow, a perpetual mourner, drooped;
And there the gadding woodbine crept about,
And there the ancient ivy. From the spot
Where the sweet maiden, in her blossoming years
Cut off, was laid with streaming eyes, and hands
That trembled as they placed her there, the rose
Sprung modest, on bowed stalk, and better spoke
Her graces, than the proudest monument.
There children set about their playmate's grave
The pansy. On the infant's little bed,
Wet at its planting with maternal tears,
Emblem of early sweetness, early death,
Nestled the lowly primrose. Childless dames,

And maids that would not raise the reddened
    eye—
Orphans, from whose young lids the light of joy
Fled early,—silent lovers, who had given
All that they lived or to the arms of earth,
Came often, o'er the recent graves to strew
Their offerings, rue, and rosemary, and flowers.

    The pilgrim bands who passed the sea to keep
Their Sabbaths in the eye of God alone,
In his wide temple of the wilderness,
Brought not these simple customs of the heart
With them. It might be, while they laid their
    dead
By the vast solemn skirts of the old groves,
And the fresh virgin soil poured forth strange
    flowers
About their graves; and the familiar shades
Of their own native isle, and wonted blooms,
And herbs were wanting, which the pious hand
Might plant or scatter there, these gentle rites
Passed out of use. Now, they are scarcely
    known,
And rarely in our borders may you meet
The tall larch, sighing in the burying-place,
Or willow, trailing low its boughs to hide
The gleaming marble. Naked rows of graves
And melancholy ranks of monuments

Are seen instead, where the coarse grass,
    between,
Shoots up its dull green spikes, and in the wind
Hisses, and the neglected bramble nigh,
Offers its berries to the schoolboy's hand,
In vain—they grow too near the dead. Yet here,
Nature, rebuking the neglect of man,
Plans often, by the ancient mossy stone,
The brier rose, and upon the broken turf
That clothes the fresher grave, the strawberry
    vine
Sprinkles its swell with blossoms, and lays forth
Her ruddy, pouting fruit. * * * * *

THE LIVING LOST.

MATRON! the children of whose love,
    Each to his grave, in youth hath passed,
And now the mould is heaped above
    The dearest and the last!
Bride! who dost wear the widow's veil
Before the wedding flowers are pale!
Ye deem the human heart endures
No deeper, bitterer grief than yours.

Yet there are pangs of keener wo,
    Of which the sufferers never speak,
Nor to the world's cold pity show
    The tears that scald the cheek,

Wrung from their eyelids by the shame
And guilt of those they shrink to name,
Whom once they loved with cheerful will,
And love, though fallen and branded, still.

Weep, ye who sorrow for the dead,
  Thus breaking hearts their pain relieve;
And reverenced are the tears ye shed,
  And honored ye who grieve.
The praise of those who sleep in earth,
The pleasant memory of their worth,
The hope to meet when life is past,
Shall heal the tortured mind at last.

But ye, who for the living lost
  That agony in secret bear,
Who shall with soothing words accost
  The strength of your despair?
Grief for your sake is scorn for them
Whom ye lament and all condemn;
And o'er the world of spirits lies
A gloom from which ye turn your eyes.

THE MASSACRE AT SCIO.

WEEP not for Scio's children slain;
  Their blood, by Turkish falchions shed,
Sends not its cry to Heaven in vain
  For vengeance on the murderer's head.

Though high the warm red torrent ran
  Between the flames that lit the sky,
Yet, for each drop, an armed man
  Shall rise, to free the land, or die.

And for each corpse, that in the sea
  Was thrown, to feast the scaly herds,
A hundred of the foe shall be
  A banquet for the mountain birds.

Stern rites and sad, shall Greece ordain
  To keep that day, along her shore,
Till the last link of slavery's chain
  Is shivered, to be worn no more.

THE INDIAN GIRL'S LAMENT

An Indian girl was sitting where
  Her lover, slain in battle, slept;
Her maiden veil, her own black hair,
  Came down o'er eyes that wept;
And wildly, in her woodland tongue,
This sad and simple lay she sung:

"I've pulled away the shrubs that grew
  Too close above thy sleeping head,
And broke the forest boughs that threw
  Their shadows o'er thy bed,
That, shining from the sweet south-west,
The sunbeams might rejoice thy rest.

"It was a weary, weary road
 That led thee to the pleasant coast,
Where thou, in his serene abode,
 Hast met thy father's ghost;
Where everlasting autumn lies
On yellow woods and sunny skies.

"'Twas I the broidered mocsen made,
 That shod thee for that distant land;
'Twas I thy bow and arrows laid
 Beside thy still cold hand;
Thy bow in many a battle bent,
Thy arrows never vainly sent.

"With wampum belts I crossed thy breast, ·
 And wrapped thee in the bison's hide,
And laid the food that pleased thee best,
 In plenty, by thy side,
And decked thee bravely, as became
A warrior of illustrious name.

"Thou'rt happy now, for thou hast passed
 The long dark journey of the grave,
And in the land of light, at last,
 Hast joined the good and brave;
Amid the flushed and balmy air,
The bravest and the loveliest there.

"Yet, oft to thine own Indian maid
 Even there thy thoughts will earthward stray,—

To her who sits where thou wert laid,
  And weeps the hours away,
Yet almost can her grief forget,
To think that thou dost love her yet.

"And thou, by one of those still lakes
  That in a shining cluster lie,
On which the south wind scarcely breaks
  The image of the sky,
A bower for thee and me hast made
Beneath the many-colored shade.

"And thou dost wait and watch to meet
  My spirit sent to join the blessed,
And, wondering what detains my feet
  From the bright land of rest,
Dost seem, in every sound, to hear
The rustling of my footsteps near."

ODE FOR AN AGRICULTURAL CELE-BRATION.

FAR back in the ages,
  The plough with wreaths was crowned;
  Entwined the chaplet round;
Till men of spoil disdained the toil
  By which the world was nourished,
The hands of kings and sages

13   G

And dews of blood enriched the soil
　Where green their laurels flourished:
—Now the world her fault repairs—
　The guilt that stains her story;
And weeps her crimes amid the cares
　That formed her earliest glory.

The proud throne shall crumble,
　The diadem shall wane,
The tribes of earth shall humble
　The pride of those who reign;
And War shall lay his pomp away;—
　The fame that heroes cherish,
The glory earned in deadly fray
　Shall fade, decay, and perish.
Honor waits, o'er all the Earth,
　Through endless generations,
The art that calls her harvests forth,
　And feeds the expectant nations.

THE RIVULET.

This little rill, that from the springs
Of yonder grove its current brings,
Plays on the slope a while, and then
Goes prattling into groves again,
Oft to its warbling waters drew
My little feet, when life was new.

When woods in early green were dressed,
And from the chambers of the west
The warmer breezes, traveling out,
Breathed the new scent of flowers about,
My truant steps from home would stray,
Upon its grassy side to play,
List the brown thrasher's vernal hymn,
And crop the violet on its brim,
With blooming cheek and open brow,
As young and gay, sweet rill, as thou.

And when the days of boyhood came,
And I had grown in love with fame,
Duly I sought thy banks, and tried
My first rude numbers by thy side.
Words cannot tell how bright and gay
The scenes of life before me lay.
Then glorious hopes, that now to speak
Would bring the blood into my cheek,
Passed o'er me; and I wrote, on high,
A name I deemed should never die.

Years change thee not. Upon yon hill
The tall old maples, verdant still,
Yet tell, in grandeur of decay,
How swift the years have passed away,
Since first, a child, and half afraid,
I wandered in the forest shade.
Thou ever joyous rivulet,
Dost dimple, leap, and prattle yet;

And sporting with the sands that pave
The windings of thy silver wave,
And dancing to thy own wild chime,
Thou laughest at the lapse of time.
The same sweet sounds are in my ear
My early childhood loved to hear;
As pure thy limpid waters run,
As bright they sparkle to the sun;
As fresh and thick the bending ranks
Of herbs that line thy oozy banks;
The violet there, in soft May dew,
Comes up, as modest and as blue;
As green amid thy current's stress,
Floats the scarce-rooted watercress:
And the brown ground-bird, in thy glen,
Still chirps as merrily as then.

Thou changest not—but I am changed
Since first thy pleasant banks I ranged;
And the grave stranger, come to see
The play-place of his infancy,
Has scarce a single trace of him
Who sported once upon thy brim.
The visions of my youth are past—
Too bright, too beautiful to last.
I've tried the world—it wears no more
The coloring of romance it wore.
Yet well has Nature kept the truth
She promised to my earliest youth.

The radiant beauty shed abroad
On all the glorious works of God,
Shows freshly, to my sobered eye,
Each charm it wore in days gone by.

A few brief years shall pass away,
And I, all trembling, weak, and gray,
Bowed to the earth, which waits to fold
My ashes in the embracing mould,
(If haply the dark will of fate
Indulge my life so long a date,)
May come for the last time to look
Upon my childhood's favorite brook.
Then dimly on my eyes shall gleam
The sparkle of thy dancing stream;
And faintly on my ear shall fall
Thy prattling current's merry call;
Yet shalt thou flow as glad and bright
As when thou met'st my infant sight.

And I shall sleep—and on thy side,
As ages after ages glide, .
Children their early sports shall try,
And pass to hoary age and die.
But thou, unchanged from year to year,
Gayly shalt play and glitter here;
Amid young flowers and tender grass
Thy endless infancy shalt pass;
And, singing down thy narrow glen,
Shalt mock the fading race of men.

MARCH.

THE stormy March is come at last,
  With wind, and cloud, and changing skies,
I hear the rushing of the blast,
  That through the snowy valley flies.

Ah, passing few are they who speak,
  Wild stormy month! in praise of thee;
Yet, though thy winds are loud and bleak,
  Thou art a welcome month to me.

For thou, to northern lands, again
  The glad and glorious sun dost bring,
And thou hast joined the gentle train
  And wear'st the gentle name of Spring.

And, in thy reign of blast and storm,
  Smiles many a long, bright, sunny day,
When the changed winds are soft and warm,
  And heaven puts on the blue of May.

Then sing aloud the gushing rills
  And the full springs, from frost set free,
That, brightly leaping down the hills,
  Are just set out to meet the sea.

The year's departing beauty hides
  Of wintry storms the sullen threat;
But in thy sternest frown abides
  A look of kindly promise yet.

Thou bring'st the hope of those calm skies,
  And that soft time of sunny showers,
When the wide bloom, on earth that lies,
  Seems of a brighter world than ours.

SONNET TO ———.

Ay, thou art for the grave; thy glances shine
  Too brightly to shine long; another Spring
Shall deck her for men's eyes,—but not for
    thine—
Sealed in a sleep which knows no wakening.
The fields for thee have no medicinal leaf,
  And the vexed ore no mineral of power;
And they who love thee wait in anxious grief
  Till the slow plague shall bring the fatal hour.
Glide softly to thy rest then; Death should come
  Gently, to one of gentle mould like thee,
As light winds wandering through groves of
    bloom
  Detach the delicate blossom from the tree.
Close thy sweet eyes, calmly, and without pain;
And we will trust in God to see thee yet again.

AN INDIAN STORY.

"I KNOW where the timid fawn abides
  In the depths of the shaded dell,
Where the leaves are broad and the thicket hides,
With its many stems and its tangled sides,
  From the eye of the hunter well.

"I know where the young May violet grows,
  In its lone and lowly nook,
On the mossy bank, where the larch-tree throws
Its broad dark boughs, in solemn repose,
  Far over the silent brook.

"And that timid fawn starts not with fear
  When I steal to her secret bower;
And that young May violet to me is dear,
And I visit the silent steamlet near,
  To look on the lovely flower."

Thus Maquon sings as he lightly walks
  To the hunting-ground on the hills;
'Tis a song of his maid of the woods and rocks,
With her bright black eyes and long black locks,
  And voice like the music of rills.

He goes to the chase—but evil eyes
  Are at watch in the thicker shades;
For she was lovely that smiled on his sighs,
And he bore, from a hundred lovers, his prize,
  The flower of the forest maids.

The boughs in the morning wind are stirred,
  And the woods their song renew,
With the early carol of many a bird,
And the quickened tune of the streamlet heard
  Where the hazels trickle with dew.

And Maquon has promised his dark-haired maid,
  Ere eve shall redden the sky,
A good red deer from the forest shade,
That bounds with the herd through grove and
    glade,
  At her cabin-door shall lie.

The hollow woods, in the setting sun,
  Ring shrill with the fire-bird's lay;
And Maquon's sylvan labors are done,
And his shafts are spent, but the spoil they won
  He bears on his homeward way.

He stops near his bower—his eye perceives
  Strange traces along the ground—
At once to the earth his burden he heaves,
He breaks through the veil of boughs and leaves,
  And gains its door with a bound.

But the vines are torn on its walls that leant,
  And all from the young shrubs there
By struggling hands have the leaves been rent,
And there hangs on the sassafras, broken and
    bent,
  One tress of the well-known hair.

But where is she who, at this calm hour,
  Ever watched his coming to see? .
She is not at the door, nor yet in the bower;
He calls—but he only hears on the flower
  The hum of the laden bee.

It is not a time for idle grief,
  Nor a time for tears to flow;
The horror that freezes his limbs is brief—
He grasps his war-axe and bow, and a sheaf
  Of darts made sharp for the foe.

And he looks for the print of the ruffian's feet,
  Where he bore the maiden away;
And he darts on the fatal path more fleet
Than the blast that hurries the vapor and sleet
  O'er the wild November day.

'Twas early summer when Maquon's bride
  Was stolen away from his door;
But at length the maples in crimson are dyed,
And the grape is black on the cabin side,—
  And she smiles at his hearth once more.

But far in the pine-grove, dark and cold,
  Where the yellow leaf falls not,
Nor the autumn shines in scarlet and gold,
There lies a hillock of fresh dark mould,
  In the deepest gloom of the spot.

And the Indian girls, that pass that way,
  Point out the ravisher's grave;
"And how soon to the bower she loved," they
    say,
"Returned the maid that was borne away
  From Maquon, the fond and the brave."

SUMMER WIND.

It is sultry day; the sun has drunk
The dew that lay upon the morning grass;
There is no rustling in the lofty elm
That canopies my dwelling, and its shade
Scarce cools me. All is silent, save the faint
And interrupted murmur of the bee,
Settling on the sick flowers, and then again
Instantly on the wing. The plants around
Feel the too potent fervors: the tall maize
Rolls up its long green leaves; the clover droops
Its tender foliage, and declines its blooms.
But far in the fierce sunshine tower the hills,
With all their growth of woods, silent and stern,
As if the scorching heat and dazzling light
Were but an element they loved. Bright clouds,
Motionless pillars of the brazen heaven,—
Their bases on the mountains—their white tops
Shining in the far ether—fire the air
With a reflected radiance, and make turn

The gazer's eye away. For me, I lie
Languidly in the shade, where the thick turf,
Yet virgin from the kisses of the sun,
Retains some freshness, and I woo the wind
That still delays its coming. Why so slow,
Gentle and voluble spirit of the air?
Oh, come and breathe upon the fainting earth
Coolness and life. Is it that in his caves
He hears me? See, on yonder woody ridge,
The pine is bending his proud top, and now
Among the nearer groves, chestnut and oak
Are tossing their green boughs about. He
     comes!
Lo, where the grassy meadow runs in waves!
The deep distressful silence of the scene
Breaks up with mingling of unnumbered sounds
And universal motion. He is come,
Shaking a shower of blossoms from the shrubs,
And bearing on their fragrance; and he brings
Music of birds, and rustling of young boughs,
And sound of swaying branches, and the voice
Of distant waterfalls. All the green herbs
Are stirring in his breath; a thousand flowers,
By the road-side and the borders of the brook,
Nod gayly to each other; glossy leaves
Are twinkling in the sun, as if the dew
Were on them yet, and silver waters break
Into small waves and sparkle as he comes.

SONG.

Dost thou idly ask to hear
  At what gentle seasons
Nymphs relent, when lovers near
  Press the tenderest reasons?
Ah, they give their faith too oft
  To the careless wooer;
Maidens' hearts are always soft:
  Would that men's were truer!

Woo the fair one, when around
  Early birds are singing;
When, o'er all the fragrant ground,
  Early herbs are springing:
When the brookside, bank, and grove,
  All with blossoms laden,
Shine with beauty, breathe of love,—
  Woo the timid maiden.

Woo her when, with rosy blush,
  Summer eve is sinking;
When, on rills that softly gush,
  Stars are softly winking;
When, through boughs that knit the bower,
  Moonlight gleams are stealing;
Woo her, till the gentle hour
  Wake a gentler feeling.

Woo her, when autumnal dyes
　　Tinge the woody mountain;
When the dropping foliage lies
　　In the weedy fountain;
Let the scene, that tells how fast
　　Youth is passing over,
Warn her, ere her bloom is past,
　　To secure her lover.

Woo her, when the north winds call
　　At the lattice nightly;
When, within the cheerful hall,
　　Blaze the fagots brightly;
While the wintry tempest round
　　Sweeps the landscape hoary,
Sweeter in her ear shall sound
　　Love's delightful story.

AFTER A TEMPEST.

THE day had been a day of wind and storm;—
The wind was laid, the storm was overpast,—
And stooping from the zenith and warm
Shone the great sun on the wide earth at last.
I stood upon the upland slope, and cast
My eye upon a broad and beauteous scene,
Where the vast plain lay girt by mountains
　　vast,
And hills o'er hills lifted their heads of green,
With pleasant vales scooped out and villages
　　between.

The rain-drops glistened on the trees around,
Whose shadows on the tall grass were not
　　stirred,
Save when a shower of diamonds, to the
　　ground,
Was shaken by the flight of startled bird;
For birds were warbling round, and bees were
　　heard
About the flowers; the cheerful rivulet sung
And gossiped, as he hastened ocean-ward;
To the gray oak the squirrel, chiding, clung,
And chirping from the ground the grasshopper
　　upsprung.

And from beneath the leaves that kept them
　　dry
Flew many a glittering insect here and there,
And darted up and down the butterfly,
That seemed a living blossom of the air.
The flocks came scattering from the thicket,
　　where
The violent rain had pent them; in the way
Strolled groups of damsels frolicksome and
　　fair;
The farmer swung the scythe or turned the
　　hay,
And 'twixt the heavy swaths his children were at
　　play.

It was a scene of peace—and, like a spell,
Did that serene and golden sunlight fall
Upon the motionless wood that clothed the
    fell,
And precipice upspringing like a wall,
And glassy river and white waterfall,
And happy living things that trod the bright
And beauteous scene; while far beyond them
    all,
On many a lovely valley, out of sight,
Was poured from the blue heavens the same soft
    golden light.

I looked, and thought the quiet of the scene
An emblem of the peace that yet shall be,
When o'er earth's continents, and isles be-
    tween,
The noise of war shall cease from sea to sea.
And married nations dwell in harmony;
When millions, crouching in the dust to one,
No more shall beg their lives on bended knee,
Nor the black stake be dressed, nor in the sun
The o'erlabored captive toil, and wish his life
    were done.

Too long, at clash of arms amid her bowers
And pools of blood, the earth has stood aghast,
The fair earth, that should only blush with
    flowers
And ruddy fruits; but not for aye can last

The storm, and sweet the sunshine when 'tis
    past.
Lo, the clouds roll away—they break—they fly,
And, like the glorious light of summer, cast
O'er the wide landscape from the embracing
    sky,
On all the peaceful world the smile of heaven
    shall lie.

AUTUMN WOODS.

Ere, in the northern gale,
The summer tresses of the trees are gone,
The woods of Autumn, all around our vale,
    Have put their glory on.

The mountains that infold,
In their wide sweep, the colored landscape
    round,
Seem groups of giant kings, in purple and gold,
    That guard the enchanted ground.

I roam the woods that crown
The upland, where the mingled splendors glow,
Where the gay company of trees look down
    On the green fields below.

14

My steps are not alone
In these bright walks; the sweet south-west, at
    play,
Flies, rustling, where the painted leaves are
    strown
    Along the winding way.

    And far in heaven, the while,
The sun, that sends that gale to wander here,
Pours out on the fair earth his quiet smile,—
    The sweetest of the year.

    Where now the solemn shade,
Verdure and gloom where many branches meet;
So grateful, when the noon of summer made
    The valleys sick with heat?

    ·Let in through all the trees
Come the strange rays; the forest depths are
    bright?
Their sunny-colored foliage, in the breeze
    Twinkles, like beams of light.

    The rivulet, late unseen,
Where bickering through the shrubs its waters
    run,
Shines with the image of its golden screen,
    And glimmerings of the sun.

But 'neath yon crimson tree,
Lover to listening maid might breathe his flame,
Nor mark, within its roseate canopy,
    Her blush of maiden shame.

Oh, Autumn! why so soon
Depart the hues that make thy forests glad;
Thy gentle wind and thy fair sunny noon,
    And leave thee wild and sad!

Ah! 'twere a lot too blessed
For ever in thy colored shades to stray;
Amid the kisses of the soft south-west ·
    To rove and dream for aye;

And leave the vain low strife
That makes men mad—the tug for wealth and
        power,
The passions and the cares that wither life,
    And waste its little hour.

NOVEMBER.

A SONNET.

YET one smile more, departing, distant sun!
    One mellow smile through the soft vapory
        air,
Ere, o'er the frozen earth, the loud winds run,
    Or snows are sifted o'er the meadows bare.

One smile on the brown hills and naked trees,
  And the dark rocks whose summer wreaths
    are cast,
And the blue gentian flower, that, in the breeze,
  Nods lonely, of her beauteous race the last.
Yet a few sunny days, in which the bee
  Shall murmur by the hedge that skirts the way,
The cricket chirp upon the russet lea,
  And man delight to linger in thy ray.
Yet one rich smile, and we will try to bear
The piercing winter frost, and winds, and dark-
  ened air.

SONG OF THE GREEK AMAZON.

I BUCKLE to my slender side
  The pistol and the scimitar,
And in my maiden flower and pride
  Am come to share the tasks of war.
And yonder stands my fiery steed,
  That paws the ground and neighs to go,
My charger of the Arab breed,—
  I took him from the routed foe.

My mirror is the mountain spring,
  At which I dress my ruffled hair;
My dimmed and dusty arms I bring,
  And wash away the blood-stain there.

Why should I guard from wind and sun
  This cheek, whose virgin rose is fled?
It was for one—oh, only one—
  I kept its bloom, and he is dead.

But they who slew him—unaware
  Of coward murderers lurking nigh—
And left him to the fowls of air,
  Are yet alive—and they must die.
They slew him—and my virgin years
  Are vowed to Greece and vengeance now,
And many an Othman dame, in tears,
  Shall rue the Grecian maiden's vow.

I touched the lute in better days,
  I led in dance the joyous band;
Ah! they may move to mirthful lays
  Whose hands can touch a lover's hand.
The march of hosts that haste to meet
  Seems gayer than the dance to me;
The lute's sweet tones are not so sweet
  As the fierce shout of victory.

THE MURDERED TRAVELER.

WHEN spring, to woods and wastes around,
  Brought bloom and joy again,
The murdered traveler's bones were found,
  Far down a narrow glen.

The fragrant birch, above him, hung
　　Her tassels in the sky;
And many a vernal blossom sprung,
　　And nodded careless by.

The red-bird warbled, as he wrought
　　His hanging nest o'erhead,
And fearless, near the fatal spot,
　　Her young the partridge led.

But there was weeping far away,
　　And gentle eyes, for him,
With watching many an anxious day,
　　Were sorrowful and dim.

They little knew, who loved him so,
　　The fearful death he met,
When shouting o'er the desert snow,
　　Unarmed, and hard beset;—

Nor how, when round the frosty pole
　　The northern dawn was red,
The mountain wolf and wild-cat stole
　　To banquet on the dead;—

Nor how, when strangers found his bones,
　　They dressed the hasty bier,
And marked his grave with nameless stones,
　　Unmoistened by a tear.

But long they looked, and feared, and wept,
  Within his distant home;
And dreamed, and started as they slept,
  For joy that he was come.

Long, long they looked—but never spied
  His welcome step again,
Nor knew the fearful death he died
  Far down that narrow glen.

JUNE.

I GAZED upon the glorious sky
    And the green mountains round;
And thought that when I came to lie
    Within the silent ground,
'Twere pleasant, that in flowery June,
When brooks send up a cheerful tune,
    And groves a joyous sound,
The sexton's hand, my grave to make,
The rich, green mountain turf should break.

A cell within the frozen mould,
    A coffin borne through sleet,
And icy clouds above it rolled,
    While fierce the tempests beat—
Away!—I will not think of these—
Blue be the sky and soft the breeze,
    Earth green beneath the feet,
And be the damp mould gently pressed
Into my narrow place of rest.

There through the long, long summer hours,
 The golden light should lie,
And thick young herbs and groups of flowers
 Stand in their beauty by.
The oriole should build and tell
His love-tale close beside my cell;
 The idle butterfly
Should rest him there, and there be heard
The housewife bee and humming-bird.

And what if cheerful shouts at noon
 Come, from the village sent,
Or songs of maids, beneath the moon
 With fairy laughter blent?
And what if, in the evening light,
Betrothed lovers walk in sight
 Of my low monument?
I would the lovely scene around
Might know no sadder sight nor sound.

I know, I know I should not see
 The season's glorious show,
Nor would its brightness shine for me,
 Nor its wild music flow;
But if, around my place of sleep,
The friends I love should come to weep,
 They might not haste to go.
Soft airs, and song, and light, and bloom,
Should keep them lingering by my tomb.

These to their softened hearts should bear
   The thought of what has been,
And speak of one who. cannot share
   The gladness of the scene;
Whose part, in all the pomp that fills
The circuit of the summer hills,
   Is—that his grave is green;
And deeply would their hearts rejoice
To hear again his living voice.

THE SKIES.

Ay! glorious thou standest there,
   Beautiful, boundless firmament!
That, swelling wide o'er earth and air,
   And round the horizon bent,
With thy bright vault, and sapphire wall,
Dost overhang and circle all.

Far, far below thee, tall old trees
   Arise, and piles built up of old,
And hills, whose ancient summits freeze
   In the fierce light and cold.
The eagle soars his utmost height,
Yet far thou stretchest o'er his flight.

Thou hast thy frowns—with thee on high
   The storm has made his airy seat,

Beyond that soft blue curtain lie
  His stores of hail and sleet.
Thence the consuming lightnings break,
There the strong hurricanes awake.

Yet art thou prodigal of smiles—
  Smiles sweeter than thy frowns are stern:
Earth sends, from all her thousand isles,
  A shout at thy return.
The glory that comes down from thee,
Bathes, in deep joy, the land and sea.

The sun, the gorgeous sun is thine,
  The pomp that brings and shuts the day,
The clouds that round him change and shine,
  The airs that fan his way.
Thence look the thoughtful stars, and there
The meek moon walks the silent air.

The sunny Italy may boast
  The beauteous tints that flush her skies,
And lovely, round the Grecian coast,
  May thy blue pillars rise.
I only know how fair they stand
Around my own beloved land.

And they are fair—a charm is theirs,
  That earth, the proud green earth, has not—

With all the forms, and hues, and airs,
  That haunt her sweetest spot.
We gaze upon thy calm pure sphere,
And read of Heaven's eternal year.

Oh, when, amid the throng of men,
  The heart grows sick of hollow mirth,
How willingly we turn us then
  Away from this cold earth,
And look into thy azure breast,
For seats of innocence and rest!

A MEDITATION ON RHODE-ISLAND COAL.

Decolor, obscuris, vilis, non ille repexam
Cesariem regum, non candida virginis ornat
Colla, nec insigni splendet per cingula morsu.
Sed nova si nigri videas miracula saxi,
Tunc superat pulchros cultus et quicquid Eois
Indus litoribus rubrâ scrutatur in algâ.
CLAUDIAN.

I SAT beside the glowing grate, fresh heaped
  With Newport coal, and as the flame grew
      bright   .
—The many-colored flame—and played and
      leaped,
  I thought of rainbows and the northern light,
Moore's Lalla Rookh, the Treasury Report,
And other brilliant matters of the sort.

And last I thought of that fair isle which sent
  The mineral fuel; on a summer day
I saw it once, with heat and travel spent,
  And scratched by dwarf-oaks in the hollow
      way;
Now dragged through sand, now jolted over
      stone—
A rugged road through rugged Tiverton.

And hotter grew the air, and hollower grew
  The deep-worn path, and horror-struck, I
      thought,
Where will this dreary passage lead me to?
  This long dull road, so narrow, deep, and hot?
I looked to see it dive in earth outright;
I looked—but saw a far more welcome sight.

Like a soft mist upon the evening shore,
  At once a lovely isle before me lay,
Smooth and with tender verdure covered o'er,
  As if just risen from its calm inland bay;
Sloped each way gently to the grassy edge,
And the small waves that dallied with the sedge.

The barley was just reaped—its heavy sheaves
  Lay on the stubble field—the tall maize stood
Dark in its summer growth, and shook its
      leaves—

And bright the sunlight played on the young
    wood—
For fifty years ago, the old men say,
The Briton hewed their ancient groves away.

I saw where fountains freshened the green land,
    And where the pleasant road, from door to
      door,
With rows of cherry-trees on either hand,
    Went wandering all that fertile region o'er—
Rogue's Island once—but when the rogues were
    dead,
Rhode Island was the name it took instead.

Beautiful island! then it only seemed
    A lovely stranger—it has grown a friend.
I gazed on its smooth slopes, but never dreamed
    How soon that bright magnificent isle would
      send
The treasures of its womb across the sea,
To warm a poet's room and boil his tea.

Dark anthracite! that reddenest on my hearth,
    Thou in those island mines didst slumber long;
But now thou art come forth to move the earth,
    And put to shame the men that mean thee
      wrong.
Thou shalt be coals of fire to those that hate
    thee,
And warm the shins of all that underrate thee.

Yea, they did wrong thee foully—they who
    mocked
  Thy honest face, and said thou wouldst not
    burn;
Of hewing thee to chimney-pieces talked,
  And grew profane—and swore, in bitter scorn,
That men might to thy inner caves retire,
And there, unsinged, abide the day of fire.

Yet is thy greatness nigh. I pause to state,
  That I too have seen greatness—even I—
Shook hands with Adams—stared at La Fayette,
  When, barehead, in the hot noon of July,
He would not let the umbrella be held o'er him,
For which three cheers burst from the mob
    before him.

And I have seen—not many months ago—
  An eastern Governor in chapeau bras
And military coat, a glorious show!
  Ride forth to visit the reviews, and ah!
How oft he smiled and bowed to Jonathan!
How many hands were shook and votes were
    won!

'Twas a great Governor—thou too shalt be
  Great in thy turn—and wide shall spread thy
    fame,

And swiftly; farthest Maine shall hear of thee,
  And cold New Brunswick gladden at thy
    name,
And, faintly through its sleets, the weeping isle
That sends the Boston folks their cod shall smile.

For thou shalt forge vast railways, and shalt heat
  The hissing rivers into steam, and drive
Huge masses from thy mines, on iron feet,
  Walking their steady way, as if alive,
Northward, till everlasting ice besets thee,
And south as far as the grim Spaniard lets thee.

Thou shalt make mighty engines swim the sea,
  Like its own monsters—boats that for a guinea
Will take a man to Havre—and shalt be
  The moving soul of many a spinning-jenny,
And ply thy shuttles, till a bard can wear
As good a suit of broadcloth as the mayor.

Then we will laugh at winter when we hear
  The grim old churl about our dwellings rave:
Thou, from that "ruler of the inverted year,"
  Shalt pluck the knotty sceptre Cowper gave,
And pull him from his sledge, and drag him in,
And melt the icicles from off his chin.

THE NEW MOON.

WHEN, as the garish day is done,
Heaven burns with the descended sun,
    'Tis passing sweet to mark,
Amid that flush of crimson light,
The new moon's modest bow grow bright,
    As earth and sky grow dark.

Few are the hearts too cold to feel
A thrill of gladness o'er them steal,
    When first the wandering eye
Sees faintly, in the evening blaze,
That glimmering curve of tender rays
    Just planted in the sky.

The sight of that young crescent brings
Thoughts of all fair and youthful things—
    The hopes of early years;
And childhood's purity and grace,
And joys that like a rainbow chase
    The passing shower of tears.

The captive yields him to the dream
Of freedom, when that virgin beam
    Comes out upon the air:
And painfully the sick man tries
To fix his dim and burning eyes
    On the soft promise there.

. Most welcome to the lover's sight,
Glitters that pure, emerging light;
    For prattling poets say,
    That sweetest is the lovers' walk,
And tenderest is their murmured talk,
    Beneath its gentle ray.

And there do graver men behold
A type of errors, loved of old,
    Forsaken and forgiven;
And thoughts and wishes not of earth,
Just opening in their early birth,
    Like that new light in heaven.

OCTOBER.

A SONNET.

Ay, thou art welcome, heaven's delicious breath,
  When woods begin to wear the crimson leaf,
  And suns grow meek, and the meek suns grow
    brief,
And the year smiles as it draws near its death.
Wind of the sunny south! oh still delay
  In the gay woods and in the golden air,
  Like to a good old age released from care,
Journeying, in long serenity, away.

15   II

In such a bright, late quiet, would that I
  Might wear out life like thee, mid bowers and
    brooks,
  And, dearer yet, the sunshine of kind looks,
And music of kind voices ever nigh;
And when my last sand twinkled in the glass,
Pass silently from men, as thou dost pass.

THE DAMSEL OF PERU.

Where olive leaves were twinkling in every
  wind that blew,
There sat beneath the pleasant shade a damsel
  of Peru.
Betwixt the slender boughs, as they opened to
  the air,
Came glimpses of her ivory neck and of her
  glossy hair;
And sweetly rang her silver voice, within that
  shady nook,
As from the shrubby glen is heard the sound of
  hidden brook.

'Tis a song of love and valor, in the noble
  Spanish tongue,
That once upon the sunny plains of old Castile
  was sung;

When, from their mountain holds, on the
    Moorish rout below,
Had rushed the Christians like a flood, and
    swept away the foe.
Awhile that melody is still, and then breaks forth
    anew
A wilder rhyme, a livelier note, of freedom and
    Peru.

For she has bound the sword to a youthful
    lover's side,
And sent him to the war the day she should have
    been his bride,
And bade him bear a faithful heart to battle for
    the right,
And held the fountains of her eyes till he was
    out of sight.
Since the parting kiss was given, six weary
    months are fled,
And yet the foe is in the land, and blood must
    yet be shed.

A white hand parts the branches, a lovely face
    looks forth,
And bright dark eyes gaze steadfastly and sadly
    toward the north.
Thou look'st in vain, sweet maiden, the sharpest
    sight would fail
To spy a sign of human life abroad in all the
    vale;

For the noon is coming on, and the sunbeams
    fiercely beat,
And the silent hills and forest-tops seem reeling
    in the heat.

That white hand is withdrawn, that fair sad face
    is gone,
But the music of that silver voice is flowing
    sweetly on,
Not as of late, in cheerful tones, but mournfully
    and low,—
A ballad of a tender maid heart-broken long
    ago,
Of him who died in battle, the youthful and the
    brave,
And her who died of sorrow, upon his early
    grave.

But see, along that mountain's slope, a fiery
    horseman ride;
Mark his torn plume, his tarnished belt, the
    sabre at his side.
His spurs are buried rowel-deep, he rides with
    loosened rein,
There's blood upon his charge 's flank and foam
    upon the mane;
He speeds him toward the olive-grove, along
    that shaded hill:
God shield the helpless maiden there, if he
    should mean her ill!

And suddenly that song has ceased, and sud-
    denly I hear
A shriek sent up amid the shade, a shriek—but
    not of fear.
For tender accents follow, and tender pauses
    speak
The overflow of gladness, when words are all
    too weak:
"I lay my good sword at thy feet, for now Peru
    is free,
And I am come to dwell beside the olive-grove
    with thee."

THE AFRICAN CHIEF.

CHAINED in the market-place he stood,
    A man of giant frame,
Amid the gathering multitude
    That shrunk to hear his name—
All stern of look and strong of limb,
    His dark eye on the ground:—
And silently they gazed on him,
    As on a lion bound.

Vainly, but well, that chief had fought,
    He was a captive now,
Yet pride, that fortune humbles not,
    Was written on his brow.

The scars his dark broad bosom wore,
    Showed warrior true and brave;
A prince among his tribe before,
    He could not be a slave.

Then to his conqueror he spake—
    "My brother is a king;
Undo this necklace from my neck,
    And take this bracelet ring,
And send me where my brother reigns,
    And I will fill thy hands
With store of ivory from the plains,
    And gold-dust from the sands."

"Not for thy ivory nor thy gold
    Will I unbind thy chain;
That bloody hand shall never hold
    The battle-spear again.
A price thy nation never gave
    Shall yet be paid for thee;
For thou shalt be the Christian's slave,
    In lands beyond the sea.".

Then wept the warrior chief, and bade
    To shred his locks away;
And one by one, each heavy braid
    Before the victor lay.
Thick were the platted locks, and long,
    And closely hidden there
Shone many a wedge of gold among
    The dark and crisped hair.

"Look, feast thy greedy eye with gold
　　Long kept for sorest need:
Take it—thou askest sums untold,
　　And say that I am freed.
Take it—my wife, the long, long day,
　　Weeps by the cocoa-tree,
And my young children leave their play,
　　And ask in vain for me."

"I take thy gold—but I have made
　　Thy fetters fast and strong,
And ween that by the cocoa shade
　　Thy wife will wait thee long."
Strong was the agony that shook
　　The captive's frame to hear,
And the proud meaning of his look
　　Was changed to mortal fear.

His heart was broken—crazed his brain:
　　At once his eye grew wild;
He struggled fiercely with his chain,
　　Whispered, and wept, and smiled;
Yet wore not long those fatal bands,
　　And once, at shut of day,
They drew him forth upon the sands,
　　The foul hyena's prey.

SPRING IN TOWN.

THE country ever has a lagging Spring,
  Waiting for May to call its violets forth,
And June its roses—showers and sunshine bring,
  Slowly, the deepening verdure o'er the earth;
To put their foliage out, the woods are slack,
And one by one the singing-birds come back.

Within the city's bounds the time of flowers
  Come earlier. Let a mild and sunny day,
Such as full often, for a few bright hours,
    Breathes through the sky of March the airs of
      May,
Shine on our roofs and chase the wintry gloom—
And lo! our borders glow with sudden bloom.

For the wide sidewalks of Broadway are then
  Gorgeous as are a rivulet's banks in June,
That overhung with blossoms, through its glen,
  Slides soft away beneath the sunny noon,
And they who search the untrodden wood for
    flowers
Meet in its depths no lovelier ones than ours.

For here are eyes that shame the violet,
  Or the dark drop that on the pansy lies,

And foreheads, white, as when in clusters set,
  The anemones by forest fountains rise;
And the spring-beauty boasts no tenderer streak
'Than the soft red on many a youthful cheek.

And thick about those lovely temples lie
  Locks that the lucky Vignardonne has curled,.
Thrice happy man; whose trade it is to buy,
  And bake, and braid those love-knots of the.
    world;
Who curls of every glossy color keepest,
And sellest, it is said, the blackest cheapest.

And well thou mayst—for Italy's brown maids
  Send the dark locks with which their brows
    are dressed,
And Gascon lasses, from their jetty braids,
  Crop half, to buy a riband for the rest;
But the fresh Norman girls their tresses spare,
And the Dutch damsel keeps her flaxen hair.

Then, henceforth, let no maid nor matron grieve,
  To see her locks of an unlovely hue,
Frouzy or thin, for liberal art shall give
  Such piles of curls as nature never knew.
Eve, with her veil of tresses, at the sight
Had blushed, outdone, and owned herself a
    fright.

Soft voices and light laughter wake the street,
　Like notes of woodbirds, and where'er the eye
Threads the long way, plumes wave, and twink-
　　ling feet
　Fall light, as hastes that crowd of beauty by.
The ostrich, hurrying o'er the desert space,
Scarce bore those tossing plumes with fleeter
　　pace.

No swimming Juno gait, of languor born,
　Is theirs, but a light step of freest grace,
Light as Camilla's o'er the unbent corn,—
　A step that speaks the spirit of the place,
Since Quiet, meek old dame, was driven away
To Sing Sing and the shores of Tappan bay.

Ye that dash by in chariots! who will care
　For steeds or footmen now? ye cannot show
Fair face, and dazzling dress, and graceful air,
　And last edition of the shape! Ah no,
These sights are for the earth and open sky,
And your loud wheels unheeded rattle by.

THE GLADNESS OF NATURE.

Is THIS a time to be cloudy and sad,
  When our mother Nature laughs around;
When even the deep blue heavens look glad,
  And gladness breathes from the blossoming
    ground?

There are notes of joy from the hang-bird and
    wren,
  And the gossip of swallows through all the sky;
The ground-squirrel gayly chirps by his den,
  And the wilding bee hums merrily by.

The clouds are at play in the azure space,
  And their shadows at play on the bright green
    vale,
And here they stretch to the frolic chase,
  And there they roll on the easy gale.

There's a dance of leaves in that aspen bower,
  There's a titter of winds in that beechen tree,
There's a smile on the fruit, and a smile on the
    flower,
  And a laugh from the brook that runs to the
    sea.

And look at the broad-faced sun, how he smiles
  On the dewy earth that smiles in his ray,
On the leaping waters and gay young isles;
  Ay, look, and he'll smile thy gloom away.

THE TWO GRAVES.

'Tis a bleak wild hill,—but green and bright
In the summer warmth and the mid-day light;
There's the hum of the bee and the chirp of the
    wren,
And the dash of the brook from the alder glen;
There's the sound of a bell from the scattered
    flock,
And the shade of the beech lies cool on the rock,
And fresh from the west is the free wind's
    breath,—
There is nothing here that speaks of death.

Far yonder, where orchards and gardens lie,
And dwellings cluster, 'tis there men die.
They are born, they die, and are buried near,
Where the populous grave-yard lightens the
    bier;
For strict and close are the ties that bind
In death the children of human-kind;
Yea, stricter and closer than those of life,—
'Tis a neighborhood that knows no strife.
They are noiselessly gathered—friend and foe—
To the still and dark assemblies below:
Without a frown or a smile they meet,
Each pale and calm in his winding-sheet;
In that sullen home of peace and gloom,
Crowded, like guests in a banquet-room.

Yet there are graves in this lonely spot,
Two humble graves,—but I meet them not.
I have seen them,—eighteen years are past,
Since I found their place in the brambles last,—
The place where, fifty winters ago,
An aged man in his locks of snow,
And an aged matron, withered with years,
Were solemnly laid!—but not with tears.
For none, who sat by the light of their hearth,
Beheld their coffins covered with earth;
Their kindred were far, and their children dead,
When the funeral prayer was coldly said.

Two low green hillocks, two small gray stones,
Rose over the place that held their bones;
But the grassy hillocks are leveled again,
And the keenest eye might search in vain,
'Mong briers, and ferns, and paths of sheep,
For the spot where the aged couple sleep.

Yet well might they lay, beneath the soil
Of this lonely spot, that man of toil,
And trench the strong hard mould with the
    spade,
Where never before a grave was made;
For he hewed the dark old woods away,
And gave the virgin fields to the day;

And the gourd and the bean, beside his door,
Bloomed where their flowers ne'er opened be-
    fore;
And the maize stood up, and the bearded rye
Bent low in the breath of an unknown sky.

'Tis said that when life is ended here,
The spirit is borne to a distant sphere;
That it visits its earthly home no more,
Nor looks on the haunts it loved before.
But why should the bodiless soul be sent
Far off, to a long, long banishment?
Talk not of the light and the living green!
It will pine for the dear familiar scene;
It will yearn, in that strange bright world, to be-
    hold
The rock and the stream it knew of old.

'Tis a cruel creed, believe it not!
Death to the good is a milder lot.
They are here,—they are here,—that harmless
    pair,
In the yellow sunshine and flowing air,
In the light cloud-shadows that slowly pass,
In the sounds that rise from the murmuring
    grass.
They sit where their humble cottage stood,
They walk by the waving edge of the wood,

And list to the long-accustomed flow
Of the brook that wets the rocks below.
Patient, and peaceful, and passionless,
As seasons on seasons swiftly press,
They watch, and wait, and linger around,
Till the day when their bodies shall leave the
    ground.

A SUMMER RAMBLE.

THE quiet August noon has come,
  A slumberous silence fills the sky,
The fields are still, the woods are dumb,
  In glassy sleep the ·waters lie.

And mark yon soft white clouds that rest
  Above our vale, a moveless throng;
The cattle on the mountain's breast
  Enjoy the grateful shadows long.

Oh, how unlike those merry hours
  In early June when Earth laughs out,
When the fresh winds make love to flowers,
  And woodlands sing and waters shout.

When in the grass sweet voices talk.
  And strains of tiny music swell
From every moss-cup of the rock,
  From every nameless blossom's bell.

But now a joy too deep for sound,
  A peace no other season knows,
Hushes the heavens and wraps the ground,
  The blessing of supreme repose.

Away! I will not be, to-day,
  The only slave of toil and care.
Away from desk and dust! away!
  I'll be as idle as the air.

Beneath the open sky abroad,   .
  Among the plants and breathing things,
The sinless, peaceful works of God,
  I'll share the calm the season brings.

Come, thou, in whose soft eyes I see
  The gentle meanings of thy heart,
One day amid the woods with me,
  From men and all their cares apart.

And where, upon the meadow's breast,
  The shadow of the thicket lies,
The blue wild flowers thou gatherest
  Shall glow yet deeper near thine eyes.

Come, and when mid the calm profound,
  I turn, those gentle eyes to seek,
They, like the lovely landscape round,
  Of innocence and peace shall speak.

Rest here, beneath the unmoving shade,
And on the silent valleys gaze,
Winding and widening, till they fade
In yon soft ring of summer haze.

The village trees their summits rear
Still as its spire, and yonder flock
At rest in those calm fields appear
As chiseled from the lifeless rock.

One tranquil mount the scene o'erlooks—
There the hushed winds their sabbath keep,
While a near hum from bees and brooks
Comes faintly like the breath of sleep.

Well may the gazer deem that when,
Worn with the struggle and the strife,
And heart-sick at the wrongs of men,
The good forsakes the scene of life;

Like this deep quiet that, awhile,
Lingers the lovely landscape o'er,
Shall be the peace whose holy smile
Welcomes him to a happier shore.

16

A SCENE ON THE BANKS OF THE HUDSON.

Cool shades and dews are round my way,
And silence of the early day;
Mid the dark rocks that watch his bed,
Glitters the mighty Hudson spread,
Unrippled, save by drops that fall
From shrubs that fringe his mountain wall;
And o'er the clear still water swells
The music of the Sabbath bells.

All, save this little nook of land
Circled with trees on which I stand;
All, save that line of hills which lie
Suspended in the mimic sky—
Seems a blue void, above, below,
Through which the white clouds come and go,
And from the green world's farthest steep
I gaze into the airy deep.

Loveliest of lovely things are they,
On earth, that soonest pass away.
The rose that lives its little hour
Is prized beyond the sculptured flower.
Even love, long tried and cherished long,
Becomes more tender and more strong,
At thought of that insatiate grave
From which its yearnings cannot save.

River! in this still hour thou hast
Too much of heaven on earth to last;
Nor long may thy still waters lie,
An image of the glorious sky.
Thy fate and mine are not repose,
And ere another evening close,
Thou to thy tides shalt turn again,
And I to seek the crowd of men.

WILLIAM TELL.

A SONNET.

CHAINS may subdue the feeble spirit, but thee,
  TELL, of the iron heart! they could not tame!
  For thou wert of the mountains; they proclaim
The everlasting creed of liberty.
That creed is written on the untrampled snow,
  Thundered by torrents which no power can
    hold,
  Save that of God, when he sends forth his
    cold,
And breathed by winds that through the free
  heaven blow.
Thou, while thy prison walls were dark around,
  Didst meditate the lesson Nature taught,
  And to thy brief captivity was brought
A vision of thy Switzerland unbound.
  The bitter cup they mingled, strengthened
    thee
  For the great work to set thy country free.

THE HUNTER'S SERENADE.

THY bower is finished, fairest!
  Fit bower for hunter's bride—
Where old woods overshadow
  The green savanna's side.
I've wandered long, and wandered far,
  And never have I met
In all this lovely western land,
  A spot so lovely yet.
But I shall think it fairer,
  When thou art come to bless,
With thy sweet smile and silver voice,
  Its silent loveliness.

For thee the wild grape glistens,
  On sunny knoll and tree,
The slim papaya ripens
  Its yellow fruit for thee.
For thee the duck, on glassy stream,
  The prairie-fowl shall die,
My rifle for thy feast shall bring
  The wild swan from the sky.
The forest's leaping panther,
  Fierce, beautiful, and fleet,
Shall yield his spotted hide to be
  A carpet for thy feet.

I know, for thou hast told me,
  Thy maiden love of flowers;
Ah, those that deck thy gardens
  Are pale compared with ours.
When our wide woods and mighty lawns
  Bloom to the April skies,
The earth has no more gorgeous sight
  To show to human eyes.
In meadows red with blossoms,
  All summer long, the bee
Murmurs, and loads his yellow thighs,
  For thee, my love, and me.

Or wouldst thou gaze at tokens
  Of ages long ago—
Our old oaks stream with mosses,
  And sprout with mistletoe;
And mighty vines, like serpents, climb
  The giant sycamore;
And trunks, o'erthrown for centuries,
  Cumber the forest floor;
And in the great savanna,
  The solitary mound,
Built by the elder world, o'erlooks
  The loneliness around.

Come, thou hast not forgotten
  Thy pledge and promise quite,
With many blushes murmured,
  Beneath the evening light.

Come, the young violets crowd my door,
  Thy earliest look to win,
And at my silent window-sill
  The jessamine peeps in.
All day the red-bird warbles,
  Upon the mulberry near,
And the night-sparrow trills her song,
  All night, with none to hear.

THE GREEK BOY.

GONE are the glorious Greeks of old,
  Glorious in mien and mind;
Their bones are mingled with the mould,
  Their dust is on the wind;
The forms they hewed from living stone
Survive the waste of years, alone,
And, scattered with their ashes, show
What greatness perished long ago.

Yet fresh the myrtles there—the springs
  Gush brightly as of yore;
Flowers blossom from the dust of kings,
  As many an age before.
There nature moulds as nobly now,
As e'er of old, the human brow;
And copies still the martial form
That braved Platæa's battle storm.

Boy! thy first looks were taught to seek
    Their heaven in Hellas' skies;
Her airs have tinged thy dusky cheek,
    Her sunshine lit thine eyes;
Thine ears have drunk the woodland strains
Heard by old poets, and thy veins
Swell with the blood of demigods,
That slumber in thy country's sods.

Now is thy nation free—though late—
    Thy elder brethren broke—
Broke, ere thy spirit felt its weight,
    The intolerable yoke.
And Greece, decayed, dethroned, doth see
Her youth renewed in such as thee:
A shoot of that old vine that made
The nations silent in its shade.

THE PAST.

    Thou unrelenting Past!
Strong are the barriers round thy dark domain,
    And fetters, sure and fast,
Hold all that enter thy unbreathing reign.

    Far in thy realm withdrawn
Old empires sit in sullenness and gloom,
    And glorious ages gone
Lie deep within the shadow of thy womb.

Chidhood, with all its mirth,
Youth, Manhood, Age, that draws us to the
  ground,
  And last, Man's Life on earth,
Glide to thy dim dominions, and are bound.

  Thou hast my better years,
Thou hast my earlier friends—the good—the
  kind,
  Yielded to thee with tears—
The venerable form—the exalted mind.

  My spirit yearns to bring
The lost ones back—yearns with desire intense,
  And struggles hard to wring
Thy bolts apart, and pluck thy captives thence.

  In vain—thy gates deny
All passage save to those who hence depart;
  Nor to the streaming eye
Thou giv'st them back—nor to the broken heart.

  In thy abysses hide
Beauty and excellence unknown—to thee
  Earth's wonder and her pride
Are gathered, as the waters to the sea;

  Labours of good to man,
Unpublished charity, unbroken faith,—
  Love, that midst grief began,
And grew with years, and faltered not in death.

Full many a mighty name
Lurks in thy depths, unuttered, unrevered;
　With thee are silent fame,
Forgotten arts, and wisdom disappeared.

　Thine for a space are they—
Yet shalt thou yield thy treasures up at last;
　Thy gates shall yet give way,
Thy bolts shall fall, inexorable Past!

　All that of good and fair
Has gone into thy womb from earliest time,
　Shall then come forth to wear
The glory and the beauty of its prime.

　They have not perished—no!
Kind words, remembered voices once so sweet,
　Smiles, radiant long ago,
And features, the great soul's apparent seat.

　All shall come back, each tie
Of pure affection shall be knit again;
　Alone shall Evil die,
And Sorrow dwell a prisoner in thy reign.

　And then shall I behold
Him, by whose kind paternal side I sprung,
　And her, who, still and cold,
Fills the next grave—the beautiful and young.

"WHEN THE FIRMAMENT QUIVERS WITH DAYLIGHT'S YOUNG BEAM."

WHEN the firmament quivers with daylight's
    young beam,
  And the woodlands awaking burst into a
    hymn,
And the glow of the sky blazes back from the
    stream,
  How the bright ones of heaven in the bright-
    ness grow dim.

Oh! 'tis sad, in that moment of glory and song,
  To see, while the hill-tops are waiting the sun,
The glittering band that kept watch all night
    long
  O'er Love and o'er Slumber, go out one by
    one:

Till the circle of ether, deep, ruddy, and vast,
  Scarce glimmers with one of the train that
    were there;
And their leader the day-star, the brightest and
    last,
  Twinkled faintly and fades in the desert of air.

Thus, Oblivion, from midst of whose shadow
    we came,
  Steals o'er us again when life's twilight is
    gone;

And the crowd of bright names, in the heaven
    of fame,
  Grow pale and are quenched as the years
    hasten on.

Let them fade—but we'll pray that the age, in
    whose flight,
  Of ourselves and our friends the remembrance
    shall die,
May rise o'er the world, with the gladness and
    light
  Of the morning that withers the stars from the
    sky.

TO THE RIVER ARVE.

SUPPOSED TO BE WRITTEN AT A HAMLET NEAR
THE FOOT OF MONT BLANC.

Not from the sands or cloven rocks,
  Thou rapid Arve! thy waters flow;
Nor earth, within her bosom, locks
  Thy dark unfathomed wells below.
Thy springs are in the cloud, thy stream
  Begins to move and murmur first
Where ice-peaks feel the noonday beam,
  Or rain-storms on the glacier burst.

Born where the thunder and the blast,
   And morning's earliest light are born,
Thou rushest swoln, and loud, and fast,
   By these low homes, as if in scorn:
Yet humbler springs yield purer waves;
   And brighter, glassier streams than thine,
Sent up from earth's unlighted caves,
   With heaven's own beam and image shine.

Yet stay; for here are flowers and trees;
   Warm rays on cottage roofs are here,
And laugh of girls, and hum of bees—
   Here linger till thy waves are clear.
Thou heedest not—thou hastest on;
   From steep to steep thy torrent falls,
Till, mingling with the mighty Rhone,
   It rests beneath Geneva's walls.

Rush on—but were there one with me
   That loved me, I would light my hearth
Here, where with God's own majesty
   Are touched the features of the earth.
By these old peaks, white, high, and vast,
   Still rising as the tempests beat,
Here would I dwell, and sleep, at last,
   Among the blossoms at their feet.

TO COLE, THE PAINTER, DEPARTING FOR EUROPE.

A SONNET.

THINE eyes shall see the light of distant skies:
>Yet, COLE! thy heart shall bear to Europe's
>strand

A living image of thy native land,
Such as on thine own glorious canvas lies;
Lone lakes—savannas where the bison roves—
>Rocks rich with summer garlands—solemn
>streams—

>Skies, where the desert eagle wheels and
>screams—

Spring bloom and autumn blaze of boundless
groves.
Fair scenes shall greet thee where thou goest—
fair,
>But different—everywhere the trace of men,
>Paths, homes, graves, ruins, from the lowest
>glen

To where life shrinks from the fierce Alpine air,
>Gaze on them, till the tears shall dim thy
>sight,

>But keep that earlier, wilder image bright.

HYMN OF THE CITY.

NOT in the solitude
Alone may man commune with Heaven, or see
   Only in savage wood
And sunny vale, the present Deity;
   Or only hear his voice
Where the winds whisper and the waves rejoice.

   Even here do I behold
Thy steps, Almighty!—here, amidst the crowd,
   Through the great city rolled,
With everlasting murmur deep and loud—
   Choking the ways that wind
'Mongst the proud piles, the work of human
     kind.

   Thy golden sunshine comes
From the round heaven, and on their dwellings
     lies,
   And lights their inner homes;
For them thou fill'st with air the unbounded
     skies,
   And givest them the stores
Of ocean, and the harvests of its shores.

   Thy Spirit is around,
Quickening the restless mass that sweeps along,
   And this eternal sound—
Voices and footfalls of the numberless throng—
   Like the resounding sea,
Or like the rainy tempest, speaks of thee.

And when the hours of rest
Come, like a calm upon the mid-sea brine,
Hushing its billowy breast—
The quiet of that moment too is thine;
It breathes of Him who keeps
The vast and helpless city while it sleeps.

THE END.

Henry Altemus Company

Altemus'
Illustrated Vademecum Series

The most popular works of standard authors, carefully printed on fine paper, with illuminated titles and frontispieces. Size, 4½ x 6½ inches.

Full cloth, ornamental, boxed, 40 cents.

ALTEMUS'
ILLUSTRATED GOLDEN DAYS SERIES
FOR YOUNG READERS

An entirely new series of copyright books, original in ideas and unusually attractive in appearance. They are thoroughly good stories, full of incident and interest, and distinctly creditable to their authors, whose names are well known in thousands of homes.

They are handsomely printed, effectively illustrated, and the binding is thoroughly suggestive of the entertaining reading within. Cloth, decorated, 50 cents.

- 1 AN EASTER LILY. *Amanda M. Douglas.*
- 2 THE PEARL RING. *Mary E. Bradley.*
- 3 BLITZEN, THE CONJURER. *Frank M. Bicknell.*
- 4 AN UNINTENTIONAL PATRIOT. *Harriet T. Comstock.*
- 5 A SHINING MARK. *William E. Barton.*
- 6 MISS APPOLINA'S CHOICE. *Ellen Douglas Deland.*
- 7 A BOY LIEUTENANT. *F. S. Bowley.*
- 8 POLLY AND THE OTHER GIRL. *Sophie Swett.*
- 9 HERM AND I. *Myron B. Gibson.*
- 10 SAM. *M. G. McClelland.*

Altemus'
Illustrated Rose-Carnation Series

A Series of Charming Gift Books

These are books for both boys and girls, with the same pleasant, readable style as happily apparent as in the previous stories of these well-known authors. Half-vellum, with illuminated sides in gold and colors, and numerous half-tone illustrations, 50 cents.

ALTEMUS'
ILLUSTRATED BEAUTIFUL STORIES SERIES
New and Copyrighted

———

Stories from the Bible told in a manner that will be readily understood and followed by young readers. These stories cannot fail to stimulate in young people a desire for a further knowledge of the Scriptures. Each has been prepared in a reverent spirit and follows the Bible narrative, with added historical information from authentic sources, when such have been available. Profusely illustrated. Half vellum, decorated in gold and colors, 25 cents.

.. 1 THE FIRST CHRISTMAS.
.. 2 THE FIRST EASTER.
.. 3 ONCE IN SEVEN YEARS.
.. 4 WITH HAMMER AND NAIL.
.. 5 FIVE KINGS IN A CAVE.
.. 6 THE WISEST MAN.
.. 7 A FARMER'S WIFE.
.. 8 THE MAN WHO DID NOT DIE.
.. 9 WHEN IRON DID SWIM.
.. 10 WHAT IS SWEETER THAN HONEY?

ALTEMUS' ILLUSTRATED CHILDREN OF THE
BIBLE SERIES

New and Copyrighted

———

Each story is complete by itself, and follows
the Bible narrative. The language is within
the comprehension of youthful readers and
the books contain a profusion of illustrations
of a quality never before shown in works of
this character. Half-vellum, decorated in
gold and colors, 25 cents.

.. 1 THE BOY WHO OBEYED.   The Story of
        Isaac.
.. 2. THE FARMER BOY. The Story of Jacob.
.. 3 THE FAVORITE SON. The Story of Joseph.
.. 4 THE ADOPTED SON. The Story of Moses.
.. 5 THE BOY GENERAL. The Story of Joshua.
.. 6 THE BOY AT SCHOOL. The Story of Samuel.
.. 7 THE SHEPHERD BOY. The Story of David.
.. 8 THE BOY WHO WOULD BE KING. The
        Story of Absalom.
.. 9 THE CAPTIVE BOY. The Story of Daniel.
.. 10 THE BOY JESUS.

ALTEMUS' YOUNG PEOPLE'S LIBRARY

A new series of choice literature for children, selected from the best and most popular works. The handsomest and most attractive series of juvenile classics before the public.

Fine English cloth, handsome new original designs, colored pictures, 50 cents.

29 MILITARY HEROES OF THE UNITED STATES. 60 illustrations.

30 UNCLE TOM'S CABIN. 90 illustrations.

32 TALES FROM SHAKESPEARE. *By Charles and Mary Lamb.* 65 illustrations.

33 ADVENTURES IN TOYLAND. 70 illustrations.

34 ADVENTURES OF A BROWNIE. 18 illustrations.

35 MIXED PICKLES. 31 illustrations.

36 LITTLE LAME PRINCE. 24 illustrations.

37 THE SLEEPY KING. 77 illustrations.

38 RIP VAN WINKLE. *By Washington Irving.* 46 illustrations.

39 A CHILD'S GARDEN OF VERSES. *By Robert Louis Stevenson.* 100 illustrations.

40 ROMULUS, THE FOUNDER OF ROME. *By Jacob Abbott.* 49 illustrations.

41 CYRUS THE GREAT, THE FOUNDER OF THE PERSIAN EMPIRE. *By Jacob Abbott.* 40 illustrations.

42 DARIUS THE GREAT, KING OF THE MEDES AND PERSIANS. *By Jacob Abbott.* 34 illustrations.

43 XERXES THE GREAT, KING OF PERSIA. *By Jacob Abbott.* 39 illustrations.

44 ALEXANDER THE GREAT, KING OF MACEDON. *By Jacob Abbott.* 51 illustrations.

ALTEMUS'

ILLUSTRATED MAGIC WAND SERIES

FOR YOUNG PEOPLE

By Tudor Jenks

These stories are bright, humorous, and especially clever in text and illustration. They are fresh examples of the author's delicate flights of fancy. Cloth, decorated, 50 cents.

.. 1 THE MAGIC WAND.
.. 2 ROMERO AND JULIETTA.
.. 3 A MAGICIAN FOR ONE DAY.
.. 4 THE PRINCE AND THE DRAGONS.
.. 5 TIMOTHY'S MAGICAL AFTERNOON.
.. 6 THE RESCUE SYNDICATE.

ALTEMUS'

ILLUSTRATED FAIRY TALES SERIES

An entirely new collection of fairy tales, carefully edited for young people. For hundreds of years they have excited the wonder and admiration of children in the different countries from which they have been gathered. Cloth, illuminated, 50 cents.

.. 1 THE MAGIC BED. (Fairy Tales from East India.)
.. 2 THE CAT AND THE MOUSE. : (Fairy Tales from Persia.)
.. 3 THE JEWELED SEA. (Fairy Tales from China.)
.. 4 THE MAGIC JAW BONE. (Fairy Tales from the South Seas.)
.. 5 THE MAN ELEPHANT. (Fairy Tales from Africa.
.. 6 THE ENCHANTED CASTLE. (Fairy Tales

ALTEMUS' GOOD TIMES SERIES

Each volume contains qualities which children will be quick to perceive and appreciate, and strongly appeals to those who judiciously select what children shall read.

Cloth, illuminated covers, profusely illustrated (5½ x 7¾ inches), 50 cents.

UNDER THE STARS. Four beautiful stories from the life of Jesus. *By Florence Morse Kingsley.*

2 THE STORY OF THE ROBINS. *By Sarah Trimmer.*

3 JACKANAPES. *By Juliana H. Ewing.*

4 THE CHRISTMAS STOCKING. *By Elizabeth Wetherell.*

5 LADDIE. *By the author of "Miss Toosey's Mission."*

6 MAKING A START. *By Tudor Jenks.*

7 THE STORY OF A DONKEY. *By Madame La Comtesse De Segur.*

8 MISS TOOSEY'S MISSION. *By the author of "Laddie."*

9 A BLUE GRASS BEAUTY. *By Gabrielle E. Jackson.*

10 THE STORY OF A SHORT LIFE. *By Juliana H. Ewing.*

11 JESSICA'S FIRST PRAYER. *By Hesba Stretton.*

12 THE ADVENTURES OF BARON MUNCHAUSEN. *By Rudolph Erich Raspe.*

ALTEMUS' ILLUSTRATED DAINTY SERIES OF
CHOICE GIFT BOOKS

Bound in half-white vellum, illuminated sides, unique designs in gold and colors, with numerous half-tone illustrations. Size, 6½ x 8 inches. Price, 50 cents.

.. 12 LITTLE GERVAISE AND OTHER STORIES. With 22 illustrations.

.. 13 THE CHRISTMAS FAIRY. *By John Strange Winter.* With 24 illustrations.

.. 14 MOLLY THE DRUMMER BOY. *By Harriet T. Comstock.* With original illustrations.

.. 15 HOW A "DEAR LITTLE COUPLE" WENT ABROAD. *By Mary D. Brine.* With 17 illustrations.

.. 16 "BOBBIE." *By Kate Langley Bosher.* Illustrated.

ALTEMUS' WAISTCOAT-POCKET CLASSICS

The smallest and daintiest "classics" ever published. · Admirably adapted for holiday and anniversary souvenirs, and as a substitute for Christmas cards. Limp leather (2⅛ x 2¾ inches), 50 cents.

.. 1 RUBÁIYAT OF OMAR KHAYYÁM.
.. 2 SAYINGS OF OUR LORD.
.. 3 ROSSETTI'S THE BLESSED DAMOZEL.
.. 4 GRAY'S ELEGY.
.. 5 TENNYSON'S DREAM OF FAIR WOMEN.
.. 6 THE SONGS OF SHAKESPEARE.
.. 7 THE EVE OF ST. AGNES.
.. 8 SONNETS FROM THE PORTUGUESE.
.. 9 ON THE MORNING OF CHRIST'S NATIVITY.
.. 10 THE MARCUS AURELIUS YEAR BOOK.

For Young Readers

Embracing popular works arranged for the young folks in words of one syllable. Printed from extra-large, clear type on fine paper, and fully illustrated by the best artists. The handsomest line of books for young children before the public.

Handsomely bound in cloth and gold, with illuminated sides, 50 cents.

.. 1 ÆSOP'S FABLES. 62 illustrations.

.. 2 A CHILD'S LIFE OF CHRIST. 49 illustrations.

.. 4 THE ADVENTURES OF ROBINSON CRUSOE. 70 illustrations.

.. 5 BUNYAN'S PILGRIM'S PROGRESS. 46 illustrations.

.. 6 SWISS FAMILY ROBINSON. 50 illustrations.

.. 7 GULLIVER'S TRAVELS. 50 illustrations.

.. 9 A CHILD'S STORY OF THE OLD TESTAMENT. 33 illustrations.

.. 10 A CHILD'S STORY OF THE NEW TESTAMENT. 40 illustrations.

.. 11 BIBLE STORIES FOR LITTLE CHILDREN. 41 illustrations.

.. 12 THE STORY OF JESUS. 40 illustrations.

Gems of religious thought, counsel and consolation, selected from the most famous religious authors. Printed in a superior manner on fine paper. Half white vellum and gold, with exquisite floral sides. 25 cents.

FRANCES RIDLEY HAVERGAL.

.. 1 MY KING.
.. 2 ROYAL BOUNTY FOR THE KING'S GUESTS.
.. 3 ROYAL COMMANDMENTS FOR THE KING'S SERVANTS.
.. 4 ROYAL INVITATION FOR THE KING'S CHILDREN.
.. 5 LOYAL RESPONSES FOR THE KING'S MINSTRELS.
.. 6 LITTLE PILLOWS.
.. 7 MORNING BELLS.
.. 8 KEPT FOR THE MASTER'S USE.

PHILLIPS BROOKS.

.. 9 THE CHRIST IN WHOM CHRISTIANS BELIEVE.
..10 TRUE LIBERTY.
..11 THE BEAUTY OF A LIFE OF SERVICE.
..12 THOUGHT AND ACTION.
..42 THE DUTY OF THE CHRISTIAN BUSINESS MAN.

DWIGHT L. MOODY.

..13 HOW TO STUDY THE BIBLE.

Dainty, inexpensive volumes, very popular as gifts for holidays and anniversaries. Half white vellum and gold with exquisite floral sides, 25 cents.

RALPH WALDO EMERSON.
.. 1 LOVE AND FRIENDSHIP.
.. 2 INTELLECT.
.. 3 SELF RELIANCE.
.. 4 MANNERS.
.. 5 CHARACTER.
.. 6 SPIRITUAL LAW.

FREDERIC HARRISON.
.. 7 THE USE AND MISUSE OF BOOKS.

EUGENE FIELD.
.. 8 THE TRIBUNE PRIMER.

EMMA GELLIBRAND.
.. 9 J. COLE.
..10 MAX AND GERALD.

MATTHEW ARNOLD.
..11 SWEETNESS AND LIGHT.

EDWARD EVERETT HALE.
..12 INDEPENDENCE DAY.

SIR JOHN LUBBOCK.
..13 ART, POETRY AND MUSIC.
..14 THE BEAUTIES OF NATURE.

..15 THE CHOICE OF BOOKS.
..16 THE DESTINY OF MAN.

RUDYARD KIPLING.
..17 THE DRUMS OF THE FORE AND AFT.
..18 THE THREE MUSKETEERS.
..19 ON THE CITY WALL.
..20 THE MAN WHO WAS.
..21 THE JUDGMENT OF DUNGARA.
..22 THE COURTING OF DINAH SHADD.
..23 ON GREENHOW HILL.

WASHINGTON IRVING.
..24 RIP VAN WINKLE.
..25 THE LEGEND OF SLEEPY HOLLOW.
..26 OLD CHRISTMAS.

JOHN RUSKIN.
..27 WORK.

BY THE AUTHOR OF "LADDIE."
..28 MISS TOOSEY'S MISSION.
..29 LADDIE.

MAURICE HEWLETT.
(Author of "Richard Yea and Nay.")
..30 A SACRIFICE AT PRATO.
..31 QUATTROCENTISTERIA.

RALPH CONNOR.
(Author of "Black Rock.")
..32 BEYOND THE MARSHES.

W. A. FRASER.
(Author of "Mooswa.")

Altemus' Illustrated Holly-Tree Series

A series of good, clean books for young people, by authors whose fame for delightful stories is world-wide. They are well printed on fine paper, handsomely illustrated, have colored frontispieces, and are bound in cloth decorated in gold and colors.   50 cents.

ALTEMUS' ILLUSTRATED BANBURY CROSS SERIES

This is a series of old favorites—immortal tales of which children never tire. Each volume is printed with great care on plate paper, and contains about forty beautiful illustrations, including a frontispiece in colors. Square 16mo, half vellum and gold, with illuminated sides. Price, 50 cents each.

.. 1 OLD MOTHER HUBBARD.
.. 2 CHICKEN LITTLE.
.. 3 BLUE BEARD.
.. 4 TOM THUMB.
.. 5 THE THREE BEARS.
.. 6 THE WHITE CAT.
.. 7 THE FAIRY GIFTS.
.. 8 SNOW WHITE AND ROSE RED.
.. 9 ALADDIN; OR, THE WONDERFUL LAMP.
.. 10 ALI BABA AND THE FORTY THIEVES.

ALTEMUS' ILLUSTRATED WEE BOOKS FOR WEE FOLKS

Filled with charming stories, beautifully illustrated with pictures in colors, and black and white. Daintily, yet durably bound. Price, 50 cents each.

,. 1 NURSERY TALES.
.. 2 NURSERY RHYMES.
.. 3 THE STORY OF PETER RABBIT.
.. 4 THE FOOLISH FOX.
.. 5 THREE LITTLE PIGS.
.. 6 THE ROBBER KITTEN.

ALTEMUS' EDITION
SHAKESPEARE'S COMPLETE WORKS

Handy volume size. Cloth, 35 cents. Limp leather, 50 cents.

.. 1 ALL'S WELL THAT ENDS WELL.
.. 2 ANTONY AND CLEOPATRA.
.. 3 A MIDSUMMER NIGHT'S DREAM.
.. 4 AS YOU LIKE IT.
.. 5 COMEDY OF ERRORS.
.. 6 CORIOLANUS.
.. 7 CYMBELINE.
.. 8 HAMLET.
.. 9 JULIUS CÆSAR.
.. 10 KING HENRY IV. (PART I.)
.. 11 KING HENRY IV. (PART II.)
.. 12 KING HENRY V.
.. 13 KING HENRY VI. (PART I.)
.. 14 KING HENRY VI. (PART II.)
.. 15 KING HENRY VI. (PART III.)
.. 16 KING HENRY VIII.
.. 17 KING JOHN.
.. 18 KING LEAR.
.. 19 KING RICHARD II.
.. 20 KING RICHARD III.
.. 21 LOVE'S LABOR LOST.
.. 22 MACBETH.
.. 23 MEASURE FOR MEASURE.
.. 24 MUCH ADO ABOUT NOTHING.
.. 25 OTHELLO.
.. 26 PERICLES.

ALTEMUS' ILLUSTRATED YOUNG PEOPLE'S HISTORIES

BY EDWARD S. ELLIS, A. M.

Profusely illustrated with frontispieces, por-
traits of the great makers of history, and superb
pictures of leading events and incidents, making
the handsomest and most interesting series of
Histories ever offered for young readers.

Cloth, illustrated, 60c. each.

YOUNG PEOPLE'S HISTORY OF THE UNITED STATES.
YOUNG PEOPLE'S HISTORY OF ENGLAND.
YOUNG PEOPLE'S HISTORY OF FRANCE.
YOUNG PEOPLE'S HISTORY OF GERMANY.

NAKED TRUTHS AND VEILED ALLUSIONS. *By Minna Thomas Antrim.* Cloth, ornamental, $0.50; ooze calf, gilt top, boxed, $1.00.

THE WISDOM OF THE FOOLISH AND THE FOLLY OF THE WISE. *By Minna Thomas Antrim,* author of "Naked Truths and Veiled Allusions." Cloth, ornamental, $0.50; ooze calf, gilt top, boxed, $1.00.

A BOOK OF TOASTS. *By Minna Thomas Antrim,* author of "Naked Truths and Veiled Allusions." Cloth, ornamental, $0.50; ooze calf, gilt top, boxed, $1.00.

DONT'S FOR GIRLS. *By Minna Thomas Antrim.* A Manual of Mistakes. Cloth, ornamental, $0.50; ooze calf, gilt top, boxed, $1.00.

DONT'S FOR BOYS. *By An Old Boy.* Errors of Conduct Corrected. Cloth, ornamental, $0.50; ooze calf, gilt top, boxed, $1.00.

POOR RICHARD, JR.'S ALMANACK. Illuminated boards, 50c.; ooze calf, $1.00.

ALTEMUS' CONVERSATION DICTIONARIES. English-French, English-German, English-Spanish. $1.00 each.

BEAUTIFUL STORIES FROM THE OLD TESTAMENT. Half vellum with illuminated sides. 45 illustrations .... .50

BEAUTIFUL STORIES FROM THE NEW TESTAMENT. Half vellum with illuminated sides. 45 illustrations .... .50

BREWER'S DICTIONARY OF PHRASE AND FABLE. *By Rev. E. Cobham Brewer, LL. D.* New edition, revised, corrected and enlarged, to which is added a concise bibliography of English literature. Nearly 1,500 pages. Imitation half morocco......................$1.50

THE AGE OF FABLE; OR, BEAUTIES OF MYTHOLOGY. *By Thomas Bulfinch.* With notes, revisions and additions by William H. Klapp, Headmaster of the Episcopal Academy, Philadelphia. Large 12mo, cloth, 448 pages, 200 illustrations and a complete index......$1.25

HALF-A-DOZEN HOUSEKEEPERS. *By Kate Douglas Wiggin.* A Story for Girls in Half-a-Dozen Chapters. 16mo, cloth, illustrated...... .75

The charm of this book is the insight the author gives us into the natural life of natural people. Every girl who reads it will put the volume in her collection of permanent acquisitions.

BUMPER AND BABY JOHN. *By Anna Chapin Ray.* 16mo, cloth, illustrated................. .50

An irresistibly humorous relation of the haps and mishaps of the homeliest dog in the world, and a delightful red-haired and freckled child, whose united ages did not exceed seven years.

HOW BESSIE KEPT HOUSE. *By Amanda M. Douglas.* 16mo, cloth, illustrated............ .50

Bessie was to keep house for her father and brothers and sisters while her mother went on a visit. She had pleaded hard to be allowed to do this; but somehow many things went wrong. What those things were and how her experiences became of the greatest value to her, one must read to find out.

THE LITTLE BOY AND THE ELEPHANT. *By Gustavus Frankenstein.* 16mo, cloth, illustrated. .50

like that of "Muti Guj, Mutineer," which Kipling never would have written had he read the story of the Little Boy and the Elephant.

POOR BOYS' CHANCES. *By John Habberton.* 12mo, cloth, illustrated .... .60

Mr. Habberton's style is clear and delightful. He never preaches, but he drives home his lesson in forceful sentences which are bound to set the reader to thinking.

TRIF AND TRIXY. 12mo, cloth, illustrated... .50

A story of a dreadfully delightful little girl and her adoring and tormented parents, relatives, and friends.

CAPS AND CAPERS. *By Gabrielle E. Jackson.* 12mo, cloth, illustrated .... .60

"A happy title to a happy book. A merry chronicle of boarding-school life."—*Journal, New York, N. Y.*

DOUGHNUTS AND DIPLOMAS. 12mo, cloth, illustrated .... .60

The heroine is an energetic piece of femininity and manages an incapable mother and a fatherless family in such a capable way as to obtain the education she covets. Eventually she makes doughnuts in the Adirondacks to enable her to acquire a diploma in the University of Michigan.

SEA KINGS AND NAVAL HEROES. *By Hartwell James.* 12mo, cloth, illustrated......... .60

Boys who delight in stories of sea fights and adventures—and what boy does not?—will find in "Sea Kings and Naval Heroes" singularly realistic descriptions of famous victories and exploits on the broad bosom of old ocean.

GALOPOFF, THE TALKING PONY. *By Tudor Jenks.* 12mo, cloth, illustrated................. .60

"The talking pony is a character with whom children and other people, too, would certainly do well to have a listening acquaintance."—*The Criterion, New York, N. Y.*

GYPSY, THE TALKING DOG. *By Tudor Jenks.* 12mo, cloth, illustrated................. .60

It is hard not to actually believe in the clever dog's feats, and as to the children in the story they are really delightful. The long conversation between Gypsy and "Galopoff, the Talking Pony" is one of the most humorous and interesting chapters in the book.

THE STORY OF THE GOLDEN FLEECE. *By Andrew Lang*...16mo, cloth illustrated.......... .50

It happened long ago, this adventure of the Golden Fleece, but the fame of the heroes who sailed away to a distant land to win themselves renown forever has lived, having been told many times in story and song. Yet who could tell it like Mr. Lang, with his poet's passion for beauty, his artist's eye for color and detail?

POLLY PERKINS' ADVENTURES. *By E. Louise Liddell.* 12mo, cloth, illustrated...:.......... .60

"The girl who loves fairy tales—and that takes in most girls of our acquaintance—will not be satisfied with one reading of Polly's remarkable adventures."—*Young People's Weekly, Elgin, Ill.*

LITTLE MISS JOY-SING. *By John Luther Long.* 16mo, cloth, illustrated................. .50

Little Miss Joy-Sing, with a poppy behind her ear, is a child of the sunshine. She slept and she woke and she wished; and there is a beautiful prince, and a fox that can talk—but the book is too clever to be cut up in pieces for inspection. Mr. Long stands inside the circle of the mighty and always has large audiences.

THE RISE OF THE DUTCH REPUBLIC. *By John Lothrop Motley.* (A History.) Complete in two volumes—over 1,600 pages. Large 12mo, cloth, per set.........................$2.00
Half morocco, gilt top, per set..........$3.25

A new and handsome library edition of a grand historical work. The masterpiece of a great American historian.

MANUAL OF MYTHOLOGY. *By Alexander S. Murray.* Greek and Roman, Norse and Old German, Hindoo and Egyptian Mythology. With notes, revisions, and additions by William H. Klapp, Headmaster of the Episcopal Academy, Philadelphia. Large 12mo, cloth, 465 pages. Two hundred illustrations......$1.25

WITCHERY WAYS. *By Amos R. Wells.* 16mo, cloth .... .50

Original F.   ˙les which are a never-ending delight to every reader.

TOMMY FOSTER'S ADVENTURES. *By Frederic A. Ober.* 12mo, cloth, illustrated......... .60

"Tommy is an everyday, honest, wide-awake little fellow, who went out into the world by himself and really saw things."—*Christian Register, Boston, Mass.*

"A thoroughly breezy story of outdoor life that cannot fail to delight boy readers."—*Young People's Weekly, Elgin, Ill.*

FOR PREY AND SPOILS; OR, THE BOY BUCCANEER. 12mo, cloth, illustrated. .60

"This story of a 'boy buccaneer' is calculated to satisfy the most exorbitant demand for action, though the tone of the book is not at all to be feared. It is a good story for the holiday season."—*St. Louis Globe-Democrat.*

MOTHER GOOSE'S PUZZLE PICTURES. A volume of nursery rhymes and puzzle pictures—pictures within pictures. Full cloth, illuminated cover design .... .50

THE ARKANSAW BEAR. *By Albert Bigelow Paine.* 12mo, cloth, illustrated................$1.00

In this witty and ingenious book a little boy and a big black bear become companions in adventures that are always diverting, sometimes pathetic, but never tragic.

THE WANDERINGS OF JOE AND EM. *By Albert Bigelow Paine.* 16mo, cloth, illustrated. .50

Joe is a New Hampshire boy with "a songbird in his throat," and Little Em is his sister. The two orphans start on foot for New York to find a famous opera singer who has heard Joe's voice and told him to come to her. The strange things that happened to them on the way are so delightfully told by Mr. Paine that we come to love both the children. One should not miss a word of this book.

A LITTLE ROUGH RIDER. *By Tudor Jenks.* 16mo, cloth, illustrated .... .60

The story of a little girl, who, as Señorita Finette, the *equestrienne,* saved the fortunes of a circus during the early years of the gold-fever in California.

ANOTHER YEAR WITH DENISE AND NED TOODLES. *By Gabrielle E. Jackson.* 16mo, cloth, illustrated .... .60

The story of another happy year with Denise and her pets.

AMY DORA'S AMUSING DAY. *By Frank M. Bicknell.* 16mo, cloth, illustrated .... .50

The adventures of a little girl in a department store.

BABY BIBLE STORIES. *By Gertrude Smith...* 16mo, ornamental, illustrated.................. .50

The Baby Bible Stories carry beautiful, easily understood lessons to the wee ones. Thousands of mothers will be thankful for them.

GEORGE WASHINGTON JONES. A Christmas Gift that Went A-begging. *By Ruth McEnery Stuart.* 16mo, cloth, ornamental, illustrated $1.00

George Washington Jones, "ten years old, little, black, sensitive," tries to give himself away to a lovely young lady who would make him her page, as in the days "befo the wah." Even without the magic of the author's name in the writing world, this book will survive as one of the best and prettiest stories ever written.

MARY AUGUSTA'S PRICE. *By Sophie Swett.* 16mo, cloth, illustrated .... .50

Of course Mary Augusta is the heroine—her name in full was Mary Augusta Wing—and her aspirations, struggles, and development into a successsful business woman are told as only Miss Swett can tell them. To read it is to read a very real book.

9 780483 723559